AXIS SYSTEM
THE PATH TO THE SELF

SAMUEL TOBON

FIRST EDITION

ISBN 979-8-9991978-0-1

BOOK DESIGN BY SANTIAGO TOBON

PRODUCED BY MELANIE PERALTA

FOR FURTHER INFORMATION:

AXIS-PLATFORM.COM

"HUMAN POSSIBILITIES ARE INFINITE WHEN ONE EMPLOYS THYSELF CONSCIOUSLY."

TABLE OF CONTENTS

- The human mechanism.
- Remembering our origin.
- Psyche and Soma: The foundations of Self.
- The call to awaken.

- The acceleration of reality.
- Crisis in the human psyche.
- The connection between mental and physical health.
- The epidemic of anxiety and depression.
- The transition from physical to digital reality.
- The global society under pressure.
- The loss of inner awareness.
- Shadow: A warning to the reader.

- Human body: The original quantum computer.
- The toroidal field of human consciousness.
- Consciousness: The sensory motor spectrum.
- The three step process of sovereignty.

- The seven hermetic principles.
- The principle of Mentalism.
- The principle of Correspondence.
- The principle of Vibration.
- The principle of Polarity.
- The principle of Rhytm.
- The principle of Gender.

- The integration of the three fields of the Self.
- A framework for harmonizing Consciousness.
- Anxiety: Overstimulation without proper output.
- Depression: Numbing and energy suppression.
- Axis solution.
- The Axis system.

- Structure and stability.
- Gravity and willpower as life and death cycles.
- The real cause of modern postural imbalance.
- The science of posture and metabolic efficiency.
- Sacred geometry and the human body.
- Posture, emotional processing and mental health.
- Posture as the Axis of well-being.
- The AXIS postural solution.
- The AXIS postural exercise.
- The mysticism of posture.
- Expanding beyond the physical.

- Regulation and flow.
- The art of Pranayama.
- The science of breath: Bridging body and mind.
- Breathwork and emotional regulation.
- Integrating breathwork into daily life.
- Introduction to breathwork practices.
- Practical breathwork exercises for emotional regulation.
- Mastering the spectrum of feeling and emotion.

- Perception and narrative.
- The great misunderstanding: "I think, Therefore I am".
- Training the mind.
- The science of attention and the construction of the Self.
- Attention as the architect of experience.
- Attention and Self-narrative.
- Meditation: training attention.

- The energy field: The unifying force of existence.
- The three electromagnetic fields of the human body.
- Energy as the currency of life.
- The reality of power & influence.
- Self-responsibility: The foundation of mastery.
- The key to your true signature vibration: Authenticity.

- The vortexes of energy processing.
- The seven Chakras:
- Muladhara: Solid field.
- Swadhisthana: Liquid field.
- Manipura: Heat field.
- Anahata: Gas field.
- Vishuddha: Sound field.
- Anja: Light field.
- Sahasrara: Void field.
- The system of emotional processing.
- The mechanics of consciousness and the path of inner alchemy.
- The self-regulatory bioelectric network.
- The human bioelectric network.
- The Self and the Chakras.
- Structure of the Unified Self.
- The Vortex of integration.
- Awakening: The activation of the system.
- The gateway to Pratyahara.

- The Seven Fields of nutrition.
- The Solid Field: Nourishment through food.
- The liquid Field: Nourishment through hydration.
- The Heat Field: Nourishment through action.
- The Gas Field: Nourishment through breath.
- The Sound Field: Nourishment through vibration.
- The Light Field: Nourishment through sunlight.
- The Void Field: Nourishment through silence.
- Integration: Power through Coherence.

Acknowledgments

The information presented in this book is not mine. It is a compilation, a weaving together of insights and knowledge drawn from many sources; ancient and contemporary, scientific and mystical, oral and written. What follows is the result of study, inquiry, direct experience, and the ongoing transmission of wisdom passed down through time.

I would like to express my deepest appreciation to all of the teachers, whose knowledge, experience and guidance has shaped my understanding of human nature and built the blocks with which The Axis System was created. My intention is to pass down their teachings so that, maybe, they will also inspire you and shape the way you think, feel, move, and live.

First, my deepest thanks and appreciation to my Mother and Father, who from a young age encouraged me to ask questions about myself, about others, about nature, and about the existence of something greater. Their curiosity and integrity shaped the foundation of my own search. It's been an honor to carry their genes, and a privilege to grow with them as I continue to learn from their example. They were my first teachers, and are essential guides in my life. Los Amo!

I also want to express my deepest gratitude and appreciation to my Yoga master and Godfather, Andrei Ram, who has been present since I was a child and who has shared with me the wisdom, discipline, and structure of the Hatha Raya Yoga technology. Much of what's written in this book regarding Yoga stems from what I've learned through him. Andrei was a disciple of Dharma Mittra, a Yoga Master who was direct disciple of Swami Kailashananda, one of the first Yogi who brought the system of Hatha Raja Yoga from India, to the West. I am grateful to be part of this lineage and spread its foundational wisdom.

I also want to show my appreciation and deep gratitude to Ishmael, my teacher in art, philosophy and mysticism; who enlighted my spirit in Melbourne, Australia. Our time together played a key role in expanding my perspective on creativity, the human psyche, magick, the processes of self-realization and individuation.

A deep thank to Felipe Sanclemente, PhD, the first reader of this manuscript and one of the longest-standing guides in my life. A close friend of my parents, he has known me since before I was born and offered me, throughout my growth, a space of trust, honesty, and conscious guidance. His insights as a first reader became meaningful additions to this work; and I am profoundly grateful for his friendship and guidance.

I also want to thank the "Pontificia Universidad Javeriana" in Bogotá, Colombia, where I completed my university studies. I am especially grateful to Bobby Rosenberg, the founder of the Somatic studies program. He brought the foundations of this field from San Francisco, to Colombia, and I was extremely fortunate to learn directly from him. His pioneering work opened the door for a whole new generation of students to explore the Soma as a gateway to knowledge, balance, love, joy and transformation.

And lastly, my appreciations to Melanie, my dear soul sister and the producer of this book. Thank you! Throughout this entire process, you have been a great mirror, a catalyzer, and a huge motivation to keep moving forward! Thank you and Alex Noff for the presence, support and time you invested in bringing this work to completion. I look forward to all the future creations we will bring to life together.

Thank you to the intelligence of the Cosmos and Consciousness, thank you for its beauty, power and the perfect tunning in all creation.

To all my teachers, near and far; thank you.

INTRODUCTION

It's 2026 and we are experiencing the greatest transformation humanity has ever known. Are you feeling it?

This was the year in which AI videos, audios, images and text became almost indistinguishable from those made by humans, and now more than ever social media is being overloaded with an endless stream of information that's selectively curated for your ethnic, social and emotional profile. We have entered in the era of POST-TRUTH when real and fake information is simultaneously being presented on the same platforms, so it becomes progressively unclear what information is real, and which is not.

This shift is accelerating faster than ever before, and its effects are already manifesting in our nervous system, in our postural health and our overall vibrational-emotional state. The symptoms become evident in the way our attention jumps from one app to the next, or how our breath shortens when we realize we've being scrolling for two hours and though we want to stop scrolling, we can't. We are hooked and hypnotized by the algorithm's intelligence.

You can see this crisis in the streets and subways, where everyone is looking at their phones. In the dinner tables where families share meals, while everyone is engaging with their phones. You can even see it in schools and hospitals, where the attention should be placed in learning and healing; yet, we choose to distract it.

I was born in 1997, in Colombia a beautiful country filled with music, dance and a culture full of colors, contrast, and resilience. I had the luck of witnessing the world before the screen took over. I remember VHS tapes filled with meaningful memories, local TV channels with that one show that brought all the family together, and house parties where everybody was present dancing.

Then came satellite television with international channels, cellphones, the internet, and console games. Each innovation seemed to be bringing the family members one step away from each other. Now, as the world digitizes with our modern AI, Social Media and Quantum Computing, it seems as if we are all falling into our own, custom curated, digital enclosure.

So, as artificial intelligence takes over human jobs and human interactions become more synthetic, this question remains:

What makes us different from machines?

And my answer is:

"That we can give meaning to our actions.

And by doing so, we give purpose to our existence."

And this has been the philosophy that guides my research as psychosomatic instructor: That we, Humans, have been gifted with the power of self-determined purpose. But, to wield this power with wisdom, we must learn to hear, see, and feel within; so that we may follow the guidance of our consciousness in the exploration of the multiple expressions of our purpose and its path.

 My university studies were as actor and contemporary dancer with emphasis in somatic studies. I spent years exploring behavior and the intelligence of motion, explored how posture affects perception, how breath reveals emotion, and how touch can synchronize people into something greater than themselves.

In 2020 I was leading a Somatic Studies research hotbed in Colombia. We were building a culture of movement, awareness, and collective energy through the practice of psychosomatic workshops and contact dance improvisation. Here we were experimenting with motion as medicine, dancing as a collective ritual, and touching as a way to become more human. We explored how posture, breath, contact and attention could unlock states of awareness more powerful than any substance. These explorations lead us to understand the Body as a doorway to something sacred.

But then... almost overnight, the pandemic arrived and it all stopped. The fear took over. The screens came closer and our body, once our bridge to connection, became a source of danger, fear and tensed frustration.

I was amazed by how the world population was bombarded with such loads of uncanny information, which created a collective Mind-Body disconnection and evolved into a current of fear for real human connection. This collective crisis made me wonder: How can I remember and encourage people to explore the power of the Mind-Body practices as the doorway to the most sacred human experience?

This is why I started writing. I realized we needed a system that reminds us of the power of our nature, a system that provides us a practical way to access, wield and express our sacred nature. And so, The Axis System was created.

The Axis System is the result of years of study, practice, and deep exploration into mysticism, yoga, biomechanics, breathwork, meditation, dance and many more techniques for conscious and enhanced behavior. It integrates the wisdom of ancient traditions, with the clarity of modern understanding, offering a practical system for self-mastery, one that is rooted in the fundamental forces that govern human experience.

I'd like to clarify that this system does not reject technology. In fact, it was created as a complementary tool of inner technology, a response to the overstimulated state of the human collective. These inner tools will help one use the tools of technology more efficiently.

At its core, the Axis System is based on three essential pillars required for one to master the complex relationship between body, mind, energy, consciousness and the collective grid of creation.

These pillars are:

1.   Posture (Being):

   • The foundation of strength and balance, it determines one's presence.

2.   Breath (Feeling):

   • The flow of energy and emotions, it determines one's vibrational state.

3.   Attention (Perceiving):

   • The direction of awareness and focus, it determines one's inner conscious narrative.

These pillars can also be understood as fields: the physical, emotional, and mental fields. These fields are each a different expression of the same unified energy field, each influencing and shaping the other. To modify the state of one, is to affect them all.

Through the exploration and training of these fields, you will learn:

• How to align your posture, enhancing your energy flow and structural integrity.

• How to explore breathwork techniques and regulate emotions through expanded awareness.

• How to train your mind to perceive reality in a way that empowers you.

WHY SHOULD YOU PRACTICE THIS SYSTEM?

Because we live in an age of extreme acceleration. Technology, information, and external stimuli bombard us at an overwhelming pace. Many people feel scattered, exhausted, or disconnected from themselves. Others feel stuck, unable to access their full creative force or purpose.

However, the modern world is not slowing down. The solution is not to escape from it, but learning to master yourself within it.

The Axis System is not about withdrawal, it's about alignment. It is about developing the inner power to navigate life with clarity, strength, and purpose.

This book is a call to those who refuse to live passively, to those who seek mastery over their time, energy, and existence. It is for those who understand that life is not just something that happens to them, it's something they have the responsibility to create.

THE JOURNEY AHEAD

This book is structured into three parts:

1.   The Context – Understanding the Human potential in the context of the modern era, its crisis and possibilities. Exposing the fundamental laws of Energy, Consciousness, and Self-mastery.

2.   The Axis System – This is the core guide to train posture, breathwork, and attention techniques in order to master the body, mind and vital energy forces into unified conscious action.

3.   The Axis Future – This is the final part, in which we introduce the Chakras and explain their unified structure as the axis of the Self. We also introduce the principles for mystic exploration, and the vision we strive forward to.

Each chapter will guide you step by step, from theory to direct experience. You will learn practical techniques to integrate into your life immediately, building a solid foundation for lasting transformation.

By the time you finish this book, you will recognize that the true purpose of life is to create a path that is uniquely yours, one that resonates with the deepest truth of who you are, with your signature vibration.

This is the beginning of that journey.

The choice is yours.

ARE YOU READY?

PART I

THE CONTEXT

CHAPTER I

THE HUMAN SYSTEM

Since I was a kid, I was always amazed by the way miracles were made. Figures like Jesus Christ, the healing Shamans of the Amazon, and the Yogi Sages of India could do things that seemed to unveil the true possibilities of what a human being is capable of. That fascination awakened the curiosity that led me to seek. In a way, my whole journey started from that first impulse: the curiosity to understand how miracles were made and to unveil the science that underlies the mystery of human nature.

One of my earliest Masters, Ishmael, used to emphasize in the fact that "All magic is but science waiting to be discovered." This means that what we call "magic" only appears magical until we understand the mechanics behind it. Once we understand the science, the technique, the principles behind an act—like an illusionist—we realize that reality itself can be shaped through mastery.

With that in my mind and heart, I began to see patterns across different cultures. I wanted to understand how far human potential could go and was fortunate to travel around the world doing this research. Everywhere I went I studied the way each culture expressed their unique way of molding creation. The more I studied, the more I realized that I needed to experience this knowledge in action to turn it into wisdom; into a lifestyle that structured my time, energy and attention in a constructive way towards my purpose.

So, I started exploring as a teenager with altered states of consciousness. First, I explored my consciousness under the influence of multiple psychedelics which progressively opened my "doors of perception" and guided me into the mystical sciences of Western esoteric traditions, and authors like Alan Watts, Baba Ram Dass, Terence McKenna, and Aldous Huxley pointed me towards the Eastern sciences of consciousness. Then, I started practicing Buddhist and Yogic technologies, studying ancient mythical texts and hermetic philosophy, so I could start comprehending the magnitude and dimension of the spectrum of spiritual technologies humanity has developed.

Over five years, I conducted this research while simultaneously training as an actor and dancer, this created the perfect balance for me to expand both the physiological and psychological aspects of consciousness. Exploring artistic expression techniques while studying ancient and modern mysticism, empowered my Self to live and experience first-hand the power of my nature, the Miracles of Mind-Body connection.

These natural miracles started to manifest in small things such as:

- How my perception of time could shrink or expand at will.
- How I could catalyze the recovery process from injury and accelerate healing.
- How physical sensations could be shifted and reshaped with breath or visualization.
- How external factors like the weather condition or someone else's vibrational state could be influenced.
- How the senses could expand to the point of sensing people and nature's energy fields.

These weren't just ideas I had read about anymore. They were real, tangible experiences that amused me: Changing traffic lights with the mind, relieving someone's shoulder pain through energy transfer, assisting someone to release a negative entity, and many more expanding experiences.

As this exploration unfolded intuitively, I kept asking myself:

What is the underlying structure in all these miracles?

And how can I synthetize that structure into a system of my own? One that is not random, non-dogmatic, non-ethnic, non-dual; something that does not fight with any belief system and serves as the steppingstone for any human to develop their natural given talents and Miracle making abilities?

Because at the core, every belief system points back to the same truth:

Everything is energy, and this energy is held together by an uncomprehensible super-intelligence. This intelligence is the source and substance of all existence, it's the creative force of nature which humans are meant to receive, contain and channel into life, action, magic and miracles. This is the intelligence of THE ALL, the intelligence that is reading right now, the one that witnesses, feels and hears through every one of us! Call it GOD, The Universe, Consciousness or the fountain of life. The name doesn't matter because it's ineffable and all cultures agree on its existence, though they have fought for millennia to set its name in stone.

THE HUMAN MECHANISM

Everything is energy, consciousness vibrating at different frequencies. And in the human system, this conscious energy expresses across different spectrums of matter:

- In its solid expression, consciousness manifests as the body.
- In its liquid expression, it manifests as emotions.
- In its gaseous expression, it manifests as the mind.

So, the body, the emotions and the mind are not separate phenomena, they are layers of a unified field: The Human Energy field. This is our real body, and the key to create Miracles.

The Axis, then, is the center point, the invisible gravitational current around which all this energy organizes itself. The axis is the organizing principle of experience. It is not found outside of us, it is not what we build, achieve, or accumulate, it is our inner alignment, our centeredness, our posture in life.

"He who looks outside dreams. He who looks inside awakens."

Carl Jung -

REMEMBERING OUR ORIGIN

The human story is vast and astonishing. We evolved from apes, mammals, sea creatures and crustaceans, from bacteria and unicellular organisms, all the way back to water, minerals, stardust, and the collapse of celestial bodies. Our lineage is cosmic.

We are the living result of exploding stars. Our very elements were forged in the furnace of supernovae. We are not separate from the universe. We are the universe becoming conscious of itself.

And yet, in the last few centuries (especially after the Industrial Revolution) our focus turned outward. Technologies began to mediate our attention, anchoring it to external productivity, consumption, and performance. We began to forget the inward realm, the inner engine of self-regulation, perception, and power.

This imbalance is what we seek to restore. AXIS is not an escape from modernity; it is the response to it! A training system to navigate it with power and grace.

It is our responsibility to remember, not only our origins, but our potential. The human evolution is not finished. The Big Bang is still expanding, and we are not just passive participants in that expansion; we are active creators.

PSYCHE AND SOMA: THE FOUNDATIONS OF THE SELF

The Human system is the most intricate mechanism we know of in the universe. It's a fusion of mind and matter, consciousness and biology. At its core lies a unique integration: the non-local, non-physical phenomenon we call "The Mind" is woven into a physical structure we call "The Body", enabling it to act, perceive, and feel.

From this perspective, being Human is a dynamic interplay between two fundamental poles of experience: Thoughts and Actions. These correspond, respectively, to The Mind and The Body also understood as "The Psyche" and "The Soma". The term "Psychosomatic" (which is the core of this system) refers to the integration of Mind and Body, Psyche and Soma, Mental and Physical into one coherent and awakened Self, The Unified Human Energy Field.

But what exactly is "Psyche" and "Soma", and why do we use these terms instead of the traditional English words Mind and Body?

The modern word "Mind" can be traced back to the ancient Greek "Nous", which refers to the intellect, understanding, or reason (This seems to indicate why we have such a fixed idea of The Mind as solely "reason"). However, when it comes to the study and science of The Mind, scholars refer to it as: "The Psyche" which Greeks used to refer not just to the intellect, but to The Soul; the animating principle, the origin of perception and meaning, the witness of experience.

We are going to dive much deeper into what "The Psyche" is in the Chapter "Mastering the Mental field".

For now, I want you to understand the crucial difference between Mind and Psyche, as The Mind as something greater than just pure intellect and reason.

The ancient word "Soma", on the other hand, is the Greek word for The Body as a living, feeling entity. Unlike the Latin word "Corpus", which refers to any physical body, "Soma" implies self-awareness. A rock has a Corpus, but only living beings have a Soma. This neuro-linguistic shift can help us transform our perception of our own body, and help us understand it as a living, feeling and self-conscious organism. One that unlike a robot, can feel, react, and resist your mental commands.

Psychosomatic studies explore the bridge between these two realms, aiming to comprehend how the living experience of the body (Soma) intertwines with the living narrative of the mind (Psyche). They teach us that our human experience is sculpted not only by what happens, but by how we tell the story of what happens. Our thoughts influence how we feel, and how we feel influences our thought. In this feedback loop lies the key to healing, integration and conscious action.

When your narrative and your sensations are aligned, when your mind and body are in coherence, you enter what modern science calls heart-brain coherence. This is the foundation for vitality, clarity, and purpose.

The AXIS system is designed to awaken this coherence through the three foundational tools of posture, breath, and attention. These are not simply techniques; they are access points into an integrated human experience.

We are not merely identities. We are systems of experience, and that experience is not yours alone; it is energy, expressing itself through you.

As Rumi wrote,

> *"Yesterday I was clever, so I wanted to change the world.*
>
> *Today I am wise, so I am changing myself."*

THE CALL TO AWAKEN

To become human is to awaken. And to awaken is to remember we cannot change the world, unless we claim who we are; not just as individuals, but as living systems of energy, consciousness, and experience. The AXIS system invites you to reclaim this remembrance and express your essence through a sacred yet practical path: aligning your posture, expanding your breath, and refining your attention. This is not new. It is eternal.

As Mahatma Gandhi once said,

> *"You must be the change you wish to see in the world."*

This has always been the message of sages, saints, and scientists alike: the world is not transformed through force, but through resonance. Through alignment. Through coherence.

There's a quote by, Buckminster Fuller, who said, "In order to change an existing paradigm, you do not struggle to try and change the problematic model. You create a new model and make the old one obsolete."

This is a timeless wisdom that's also expressed, in a different way, by the great Lao Tzu millennia earlier:

"Knowing others is intelligence; knowing yourself is true wisdom.

Mastering others is strength; mastering yourself is true power."

The human system, when remembered, reawakened, and re-embodied; becomes a tuning fork for transformation. When one person awakens to their center, the frequency of that awakening spreads like ripples through space and time. Your healing is not yours alone. Your coherence becomes a path for others.

You are not the first to walk this path, and you will not be the last. This work is not about becoming something new. It is about remembering something ancient, something sacred.

Because when you stand at the center of your experience, fully aligned in mind and body, breath and will, you become the sovereign of your reality. The Master of Creation. And this book, this system, is your invitation to claim it; to look inward, to align with your axis, and to begin the Path to Yourself.

CHAPTER II

THE MODERN ERA

THE ACCELERATION OF REALITY

It is 2026 and the very structure of human society is shifting faster than ever before. Technological evolution, economic transformation, and the rise of artificial intelligence are altering not just how we work, interact, and learn; but how we perceive and experience reality itself.

We are in an era where certainty is fading, attention is fractured, and overstimulation is the new normal. Yet, for most of history, human beings lived in rhythmic cycles that matched the pace of nature.

Our ancestors told stories, then wrote manuscripts, and then invented the printing press. Each of these transitions brought significant shifts in how we stored, transmitted, and processed knowledge.

We transitioned from print to radio, from radio to television, from television to the internet, and now from the internet to artificial intelligence. The transition time between each major technological revolution has shortened dramatically, what once took centuries, then took decades, is now happening in a matter of years, sometimes even months.

We have crossed a threshold where human consciousness is struggling to keep pace with the velocity of change. The sheer amount of data, notifications, and digital stimuli bombarding our nervous systems daily has reached unprecedented levels. In a single day, the average person is exposed to more information than a person living in the 15th century encountered in an entire week.

CRISIS IN HUMAN PSYCHE

-A Constant Fight-or-Flight Response-

The modern human is no longer hunted by wild animals or natural disasters. Instead, we are hunted by a never-ending stream of information, expectations, and artificial stimulation that keep us in a constant state of hyperarousal.

Our nervous systems, designed for cycles of stress and recovery, are now trapped in a perpetual state of activation. Anxiety, depression, burnout, and emotional dysregulation are no longer personal afflictions, they are symptoms of an overloaded species struggling to process the sheer magnitude of modern reality.

For most of human history, stress was temporary. It was a biological tool for survival, helping us escape danger or respond to immediate threats. Once the threat was gone, the parasympathetic nervous system (the rest-and-digest response) would reset the body, allowing it to recover.

But today, stress never turns off.

- Emails. Messages. Notifications. Deadlines.
- News cycles designed to provoke fear.
- Social media feedback loops reinforcing comparison and self-doubt.

This chronic fight-or-flight response results in cortisol overproduction, which has been linked to:

- Weakened immune function (McEwen, 2019)
- Cardiovascular disease (Chida & Steptoe, 2010)
- Memory impairment and cognitive decline (Lupien et al., 2009)

Dr. Bruce McEwen describes this as "allostatic overload" (when the body can no longer regulate stress properly) leading to physical and mental exhaustion (McEwen, 2019).

The modern nervous system is collapsing under the weight of relentless stimuli, and our bodies are paying the price.

THE CONNECTION BETWEEN MENTAL AND PHYSICAL HEALTH

The mind and body are not separate, when one is overwhelmed, the other suffers.

Psychologist Dr. Gabor Maté, a leading expert in stress-related illness, explains: "Chronic stress does not just make us anxious or depressed; it actually rewires the nervous system, weakens the immune response, and increases vulnerability to autoimmune diseases, chronic pain, and even cancer" (Maté, 2019).

- Anxiety and gut health are directly linked: the gut produces 90% of the body's serotonin, and chronic stress disrupts its function, leading to mood disorders (Mayer, 2016).
- Heart disease is influenced by emotional stress: anger and chronic worry significantly increase cardiovascular risks (Steptoe & Kivimäki, 2013).
- Poor posture and emotional suppression are correlated: slouched posture has been shown to increase feelings of depression (Peper et al., 2017).

This means that mental instability is not just psychological, it is deeply physiological.

THE EPIDEMIC OF ANXIETY AND DEPRESSION

The human attention span has been steadily declining. In 2000, it was measured at 12 seconds; by 2015, it had dropped to 8.25 seconds, shorter than that of a goldfish (McSpadden, 2015), and data released by Meta in 2025 shows that users spend an average of 1.7 seconds on each piece of content and the average person checks their phone over 260 times per day (Asurion, 2022). This isn't just a lighthearted statistic; it is an indication of cognitive degeneration at a societal scale.

As Dr. Lisa Damour explains, "The ability to regulate emotion is one of the most important predictors of long-term mental health. When people rely on external validation rather than internal self-regulation, they become more vulnerable to anxiety, depression, and compulsive behaviors." (Damour, 2023).

Unfortunately, it is evident that as technological progress accelerates, mental health is declining. And these are some of the effects measured globally:

- A study published in JAMA Psychiatry found that clinical anxiety disorders have increased by over 25% globally in the past decade (Santomauro et al., 2021).
- The World Health Organization (WHO) reports that depression is now the leading cause of disability worldwide, affecting over 280 million people (World Health Organization, 2022).
- The American Psychological Association found that the average person now experiences the same level of anxiety as psychiatric patients did in the 1950s (Twenge, 2017).

Neuroscientists have observed that chronic overstimulation weakens our ability to focus, process information, and retain deep, meaningful thought. As Dr. Daniel Levitin explains, "The brain is not designed to process an infinite stream of stimuli. The more we divide our attention, the less effective we become at filtering what actually matters" (Levitin, 2015).

Psychiatrist Dr. Anna Lembke describes this as "dopamine addiction": A condition where people need constant digital stimuli to feel engaged, leading to increased depression and an inability to experience real-world pleasure (Lembke, 2021).

However, the digital platforms are designed to keep users engaged for as long as possible by triggering dopamine release through rapid, unpredictable feedback loops; notifications, likes, and algorithmic recommendations.

- Social media algorithms manipulate our neurochemistry, reinforcing compulsive behaviors.
- Short-form content (TikTok, Instagram Reels, YouTube Shorts) trains the brain to seek instant gratification over sustained thought.
- The endless cycle of breaking news keeps us in a state of hypervigilance.

THE TRANSITION FROM PHYSICAL TO DIGITAL REALITY

Beyond the decline of attention, a deeper transformation is taking place: human experiences are shifting from physical to digital reality.

More people now socialize, learn, work, and entertain themselves entirely online. Virtual reality, augmented reality, and AI-driven interactions are becoming the dominant mode of engagement. We are living more in the simulated world than in the real one.

- Social media has totally redefined what it means to "exist" socially.

- AI-generated content is now creating experiences that feel indistinguishable from human-made ones.
- Our digital identity is replacing the physical, tangible self as the primary source of identity.

In essence, reality itself is becoming programmable. And while this shift opens new possibilities, it also comes with profound risks:

- The collapse of genuine human connection: more people experience loneliness despite being "connected" at all times.
- Loss of direct sensory experience: physical movement, embodied learning, and real-world problem-solving are being replaced by virtual engagement.
- Algorithmic determinism: AI-driven personalization is creating echo chambers where individuals only receive information that reinforces their existing beliefs.

As researcher Tristan Harris warns, "We are moving toward a world where AI knows more about your desires than you do. The question is: are we still the authors of our own consciousness?" (Harris, 2023).

THE GLOBAL SOCIETY UNDER PRESSURE

These transformations are not just happening on an individual level, they are affecting society as a whole.

- Rising political polarization is fueled by AI-driven bots posting content in public feeds to amplify outrage.
- Economic instability is creating mass anxiety as industries are rapidly disrupted with emergent technologies.
- Trust in institutions, government and academia is eroding, as misinformation and deepfakes make truth increasingly difficult to discern.

Dr. Jonathan Haidt, a social psychologist, states, "The digital revolution has reshaped the moral, political, and social fabric of human society faster than we've had time to develop ethical frameworks to manage it" (Haidt, 2022).

THE LOSS OF INNER AWARENESS

In an overstimulated world, we have lost the ability to listen to ourselves. Instead of tuning into our own bodies and emotions, we are lured by external forces: news cycles, digital opinions, and social trends which tell us what to do, feel and believe.

The philosopher Jiddu Krishnamurti wrote, "It is no measure of health to be well adjusted to a profoundly sick society." Today, we normalize a life where:

• We are perpetually distracted.

• We feel anxious without knowing why.

• We struggle to experience presence and joy.

This disconnection from Self is the greatest crisis of all.

The modern world has rewired our nervous systems, eroded our emotional regulation, and disrupted the natural balance of stress and recovery.

But what can we do?

How do we reclaim focus in a world designed for distraction?

How do we regulate stress when everything around us is designed to keep us overstimulated?

How do we reconnect with our bodies and minds when we have been trained to escape them?

THROUGH THE AXIS SYSTEM.

The Axis System proposes that rather than passively succumbing to the crises of the modern world, individuals can take intentional steps to reclaim their own vitality. By harnessing posture, breathwork, and focused attention, we can begin to counteract the harmful effects of chronic stress, social disconnection, and economic instability; creating a foundation for a more resilient, conscious, and thriving human experience.

To reclaim mastery over our experience, we must first recognize that we are not merely individuals reacting to external forces, but a super-intelligent biosystem of consciousness, intelligence, and matter. If we fail to recognize this, we will remain at the mercy of external technologies rather than learning to wield the greatest technology ever created: ourselves.

It is not about rejecting modern advancements, but about understanding how to use them in harmony with the most powerful processor we already possess: the human system.

Through the Axis framework, we will unlock the mechanisms that allow us to:

- Understand the integrated nature of your consciousness.
- Expand our cognitive and emotional capacity to handle rapid change.
- Rewire our nervous system to process information without overwhelm.
- Synchronize our body's intelligence with our conscious awareness.
- Develop a deeper understanding of the self as both an individual and a collective expression of consciousness.

SHADOW:

A WARNING TO THE READER

The Axis system will increase your power, it will increase your vitality, your clarity, your capacity to act, and your ability to influence both yourself and the world around you. This is not symbolic power; it is real, embodied power. And with every increase in power, something else grows alongside it: your shadow.

The shadow is not evil.

The shadow is not a flaw.

The shadow is simply everything that you are, but do not yet recognize as yourself.

If the ego (the sense of identity) is built from the traits, values, stories, and roles you consciously identify with; then the shadow is composed of everything you disown, repress, deny, or fail to perceive. These are impulses, desires, fears, capacities, and tendencies that operate outside your conscious self-image, yet still act through you.

As your energy increases, your shadow does not disappear, it becomes sharper, faster, and more effective. This is why shadow awareness is not optional.

As you gain more strength, clarity, charisma, intelligence, and creative force, you also gain a greater ability to harm—yourself and others—if that power is unconsciously driven. Unexamined shadow does not stay dormant. It expresses itself through projection, manipulation, self-sabotage, spiritual bypassing, abuse of influence, and distorted intentions that feel justified.

True wisdom does not come from being the most powerful, the most capable, or the most "aligned."

It comes from knowing how to use power, why you are using it, and what within you is seeking expression through it.

Shadow work is the practice of facing what you have not yet integrated. Through acknowledgment, responsibility, and honest observation, these fragments can be integrated rather than acted out unconsciously. As you integrate your shadow, your sense of Self expands.

This process is not only personal. When individuals take responsibility for their own shadow, the collective shadow begins to surface and soften. We heal together by recognizing that power without awareness is dangerous; and that greater power demands greater responsibility (as uncle Ben said).

Be warned:

If you cultivate energy, alignment, and vitality through proper nutrition, breath, posture and nervous system coherence without cultivating shadow awareness, that same power can turn against you. It can amplify unconscious patterns, reinforce egoic distortion, and ripple outward into the world in harmful ways.

Do not seek power to dominate, escape, or inflate identity.

CHAPTER III

THE STRUCTURE OF CONSCIOUSNESS

HUMAN BODY: THE ORIGINAL QUANTUM COMPUTER

At the core of human experience is the body: A living, breathing, hyper-intelligent biological system that operates with an astonishing degree of complexity. While we often believe our conscious mind is in control, the vast majority of functions necessary for survival are executed automatically by the parasympathetic nervous system: our heart beats, our lungs breathe, our digestion functions, our cells regenerate – all without our conscious intervention.

To put this into perspective: if we had to manually oversee the trillions of cellular processes occurring within us every second, our conscious mind would be entirely consumed by maintaining basic survival. Instead, our body operates like a super-intelligent quantum computer, executing millions of operations simultaneously, allowing us to focus on higher cognitive functions.

If we wish to unveil the wonderful powers of our nature and use our system as the super biocomputer that it is, first, we must understand the layers of our consciousness.

1. The Subconscious Mind (Constant Passive Awareness) → This is the ever-present recording system of our being. It absorbs everything we see, hear, feel, and experience, but lacks the capacity

to act upon it directly. It is the reservoir of our habits, emotions, and deeply ingrained patterns.

2. The Conscious Mind (Programmable Active Awareness) → This is the aspect of awareness that allows us to make intentional choices. Unlike the subconscious, which passively records, the conscious mind has the power to act rather than react, allowing us to engage in the present moment with awareness.

3. The Superconscious Mind (Conscious Creative Awareness) → The highest state of awareness, where we not only perceive ourselves but also recognize the interconnectedness of all things. The superconscious mind is the realm of visionaries, creators, and those who see beyond their personal experience to the larger fabric of reality.

These three layers of consciousness shape how we engage with both our internal and external world.

THE TOROIDAL FIELD OF HUMAN CONSCIOUSNESS

Human consciousness is a self-organizing intelligence field, moving through continuous cycles of contraction and expansion; the dance between gravity and energy, magnetism and electricity, input and output, negative and positive charge. These binary pulses create specific vibrational dynamics that shape the expression of one's body, mind, and emotions.

Contraction occurs when consciousness feels and takes in information. It is the gravitational movement of energy, the system absorbing a bit of data from the collective field. A contraction equals a +1, a unit of information entering the Self.

Expansion happens when consciousness acts and puts out information. It is the electrical movement of expression, releasing energy outward to affect the world. An expansion equals a –1, a unit of energy leaving the system.

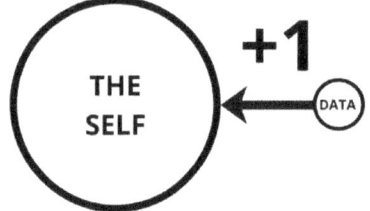
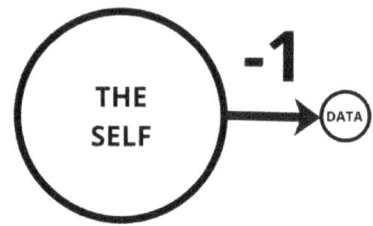

Because energy and information are the same substance moving in two opposite directions, the human being is always translating the collective field into experience (through contraction) and translating experience back into action (through expansion). This is how we alter the state of the collective matter and, simultaneously, feel its shifting state in return.

If we were to read each contraction as a 0 and each expansion as a 1, the whole oscillation of a person's consciousness could be understood as a kind of binary code, a vibrational signature unique to each individual. More importantly, by reading our own sequence of contractions and expansions, we can measure our internal charges, stabilize the system, and optimize the application, distribution, and containment of vital energy.

Every person operates with a specific vibrational frequency, and this frequency determines how consciousness expresses through the physical body, mental patterns, and emotional states.

The central magic of the human energy field is that it transforms energy into experience. This is possible because the unified field of the self is an electromagnetic toroidal structure. The torus converts raw energy (photons) into pulses of information (neural activity) through a process still largely mysterious and not yet fully deciphered, one rooted in the fundamental geometry and dynamics of toroidal energy fields.

Next you will see a graphic that depicts the geometric structure and three-dimensional shape of four toroidal energy fields in different expressions of nature, one micro, one macro, one human, and one human made.

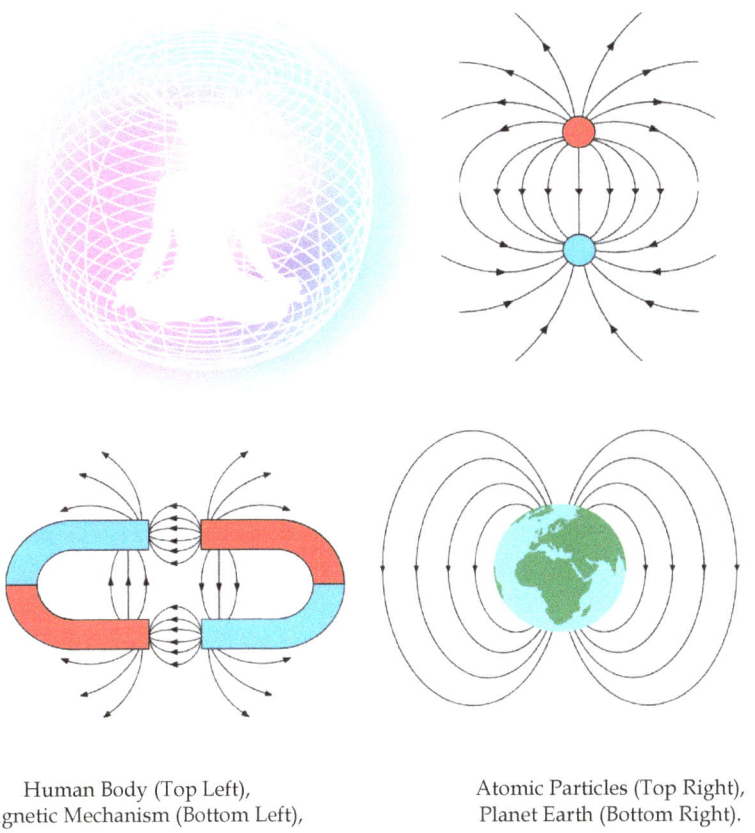

Human Body (Top Left),
Magnetic Mechanism (Bottom Left),

Atomic Particles (Top Right),
Planet Earth (Bottom Right).

In this model, balance is essential.

When one feels, far more than one acts, the system becomes overloaded.

When one acts, far more than one feels, the system becomes unstable.

The structure is maintained not by reducing feeling or action but by keeping their rhythm alive. Contraction and expansion must remain in dialogue, each movement informing and stabilizing the other.

What I love the most about Toroidal Fields is that they're not unique to humans; it is the fundamental energetic structure of everything in existence, from supernovas to subatomic particles.

You are not a separate being experiencing the universe...

you ARE the universe, experiencing itself.

So, just as every star, planet, and cell in your body operates within a toroidal electromagnetic field, so does the energy field of your consciousness. And this electromagnetic field of consciousness operates across three key states:

1. Subconscious (Soma / Magnetic charge / Feeling) → Absorbs and records experience but does not act.

- Magnetism: absorbing information through feeling and perception.

2. Conscious (Self/Electromagnetic field/Acting) → The bridge between perception and action.

- Central Axis: the balance between gravity and radiation.

3. Superconscious (Psyche/Electric charge/Perceiving) → Shapes reality itself through directed action.

- Electricity: expressing information through thought, action, and creation.

The integration of these three states is what creates the Self, the Unified Energy Field (U.E.F) that is responsible of the Toroidal Flow → the continuous circulation of consciousness and energy, absorbing data (input) and manifesting reality (output).

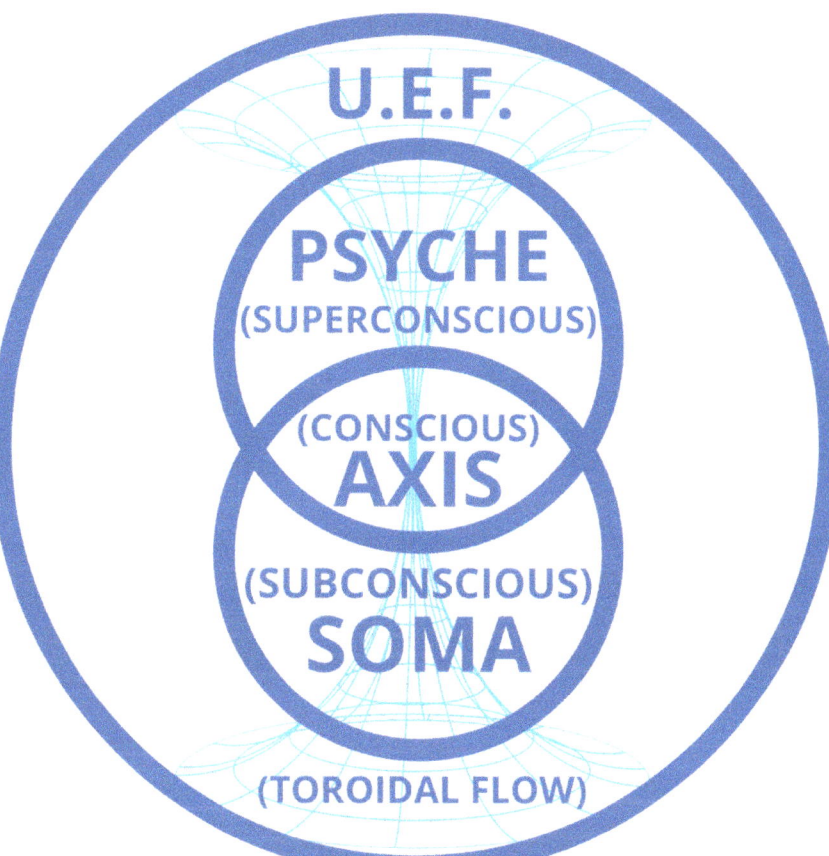

In this order of ideas, we can measure the level of vitality and resonance in an individual by measuring the magnitude of its toroidal flow. The more vital and alive one is, the more information its consciousness is able to process.

So, the more energy you process and transform from information into matter, and from matter into information, the more power you can contain within your unified energy field, and the more miracles you can create!

CONSCIOUSNESS: THE SENSORY-MOTOR SPECTRUM

Thomas Hanna, the founder of somatic studies, defined consciousness as "The sensory-motor spectrum". The seamless interplay between feeling (sensory input) and doing (motor output). This principle is fundamental to the AXIS system, as it reveals the very architecture of human awareness.

If consciousness itself is an electromagnetic field, then it consists of two polarities:

• Feeling (Negative / Inward Pull): the receptive force, the gravitational pull of experience inward. This is the negative pole of consciousness, drawing energy inward to the nucleus of the self. It is magnetism, introspection, and gravity.

• Acting (Positive / Outward Projection): the expansive force, the radiation of experience outward into motion and expression. This is the positive pole of consciousness, pushing energy from the nucleus outward into the world. It is radiation, movement, and creation.

The spectrum between these two forces is what we call consciousness: a continuous dance between sensation and action, between receiving and expressing, between absorbing the world and reshaping it.

When we feel, we are feeling the world. When we act, we are acting upon the world.

When we change the world, we change ourselves. When we change ourselves, we change the world.

There is no separation.

I am you; you are me.

Understanding this sensory-motor spectrum gives us a new perspective on how we navigate life. If we feel disconnected, fragmented, or powerless, it is likely because we are not fully engaged in one or both of these processes. Some people are trapped in an excess of feeling (absorbing emotions, information, and stimuli) but unable to translate them into action. Others are trapped in overaction (constantly doing, producing, and moving) without conscious awareness of what they are creating or why.

Mastery comes from holding both ends of the spectrum with intention:

• Expanding our ability to feel (deepening awareness, sensation, introspection).

• Refining our ability to act (directing energy into meaningful motion).

THE THREE-STEP PROCESS OF SOVEREIGNTY

1. Recognition (Feeling / Awareness)

• The first step is recognizing, which means feeling. We must expand our ability to sense, to allow the full spectrum of our emotions, sensations, and inner awareness to emerge without suppression or resistance. This requires a conscious engagement with our nervous system, an allowance of experience rather than avoidance.

2. Transformation (Decision / Consciousness)

• Once we have fully felt and acknowledged our inner state, we must choose how to transform it. Transformation is the law.

Everything is always in flux, always shifting. The power we have — the power of the Alchemist — is to determine how we transmute the experiences, emotions, and energies we encounter. Do we let fear immobilize us, or do we channel it into action? Do we let stress consume us, or do we mold it into strength? The decision to transform is our conscious act of will.

3. Action (Doing / Creation)

• The final step is execution, taking action. Feeling without action leads to stagnation, and action without awareness leads to chaos. The process is incomplete without movement, without putting transformation into the world. When we do, we do not act in isolation. Every action we take reshapes both our internal reality and the external world. There is no separation.

CHAPTER IV

BRIDGING ANCIENT WISDOM AND MODERN SCIENCE

The ancients understood what we are only now beginning to prove with modern science. From the monks of the Himalayas to the shamans of the Amazon rainforest, from the priest-scientists of ancient Egypt to the hidden esoteric orders of the West, all shared a common truth:

The universe and the human being are both fields of energy, structured by consciousness.

The theory of relativity echoes this wisdom, revealing that matter is energy vibrating at different frequencies. Einstein's equation, $E=mc^2$, states that mass is slow-moving energy, and energy is fast-moving mass. The difference between physical matter and pure light is simply the rate of frequency it is vibrating at.

This means that everything in existence is an expression of energy in motion, following the universal principles. The ancients understood these principles so deeply that they used them to build civilizations, technologies, and spiritual disciplines designed to harmonize human consciousness with the greater cosmic field.

But this knowledge is not merely theoretical, it is deeply practical. The ancient sages understood that by aligning ourselves with the fundamental principles of reality, we could master our mind-body system, expand our awareness, and even shape the external world.

The foundation of this understanding is encoded in the Seven Hermetic Principles – teachings that originated in ancient Egypt as the Emerald Tablet and were later compiled into The Kybalion, a work that distilled the esoteric knowledge of "Hermes Trismegistus" (The ancient sage that was deified as Thoth in Egypt, Hermes in Greece, Mercury in Rome).

Thoth   Hermes Trismegistus   MERCURY.

This text by The Three Initiates is one of the foundational texts for the freemasons, hermeneuts, alchemist and mystics of the West.

The principles presented in this book are not abstract philosophy; they describe the structure of consciousness itself. They reveal the holographic nature of reality, where each part contains the whole, and they show us how our awareness is an electromagnetic field that operates within the universal energetic framework.

To truly understand the AXIS system, we must first understand these fundamental laws of existence.

THE SEVEN HERMETIC PRINCIPLES

The Hermetic Principles are the underlying laws that govern the structure of consciousness and the mechanics of reality. They are known as the "Principles of Truth", and provide a framework for understanding how energy moves, how thought shapes experience, and how humans can align with the nature of existence and its laws.

"The Principles of Truth are Seven; he who knows these, understandingly, possesses the Magic Key before whose touch all the Doors of the Temple fly open."

— The Kybalion.

Each of these principles reveal a different aspect of the holographic nature of the universe, showing how everything is interconnected and operates according to universal rhythms and forces.

I

THE PRINCIPLE OF MENTALISM

"The All is Mind"

Everything begins with consciousness.

"This Principle embodies the truth that "All is Mind." It explains that The All is Spirit, which in itself is Unknowable and Undefinable, but which may be considered and thought of as A Universal, Infinite, Living Mind."

— The Kybalion.

This is not to say that the universe is a mere illusion, but rather that it is a projection of a greater intelligence, a field of awareness in which all things exist. Just as dreams emerge from the mind of the dreamer, so too does reality emerge from the infinite mind of the Universe.

Example: Imagine you are in a dream. While dreaming, everything seems real, the people, the environment, the experiences. But upon waking, you realize that it was all a construct of your own consciousness. Now, what if physical reality operated in a similar way? What if what we call "objective reality" is simply a shared field of consciousness, shaped by perception, thought, and belief?

This principle shows us that our experience of reality is created through our own consciousness. When we transform our thoughts, emotions, and perceptions, we literally transform our reality, because reality is not separate from us, but an extension of our own awareness.

"This Principle explains the true nature of "Energy," "Power," and "Matter," and why and how all these are subordinate to the Mastery of Mind."

– The Kybalion.

II

THE PRINCIPLE OF CORRESPONDENCE

"As Above, So Below"

"This Principle embodies the truth that there is always a Correspondence between the laws and phenomena of the various planes of Being and Life."

– The Kybalion.

This principle states that the same fundamental structures repeat across all scales of reality. From the macrocosm (galaxies, planets, stars) to the microcosm (atoms, cells, neurons), the same energetic patterns govern the formation and behavior of everything.

"The old Hermetic axiom ran in these words: "As above, so below; as below, so above." And the grasping of this Principle gives one the means of solving many a dark paradox, and the hidden secrets of Nature. There are planes beyond our knowing, but when we apply this Principle, we are able to understand much that would otherwise be unknowable to us."

— The Kybalion.

The spiral patterns of galaxies mirror the structure of hurricanes, whirlpools, and even the patterns of DNA. The structure of an atom (with a nucleus surrounded by orbiting electrons) is strikingly similar to the structure of the solar system, with planets orbiting a central star.

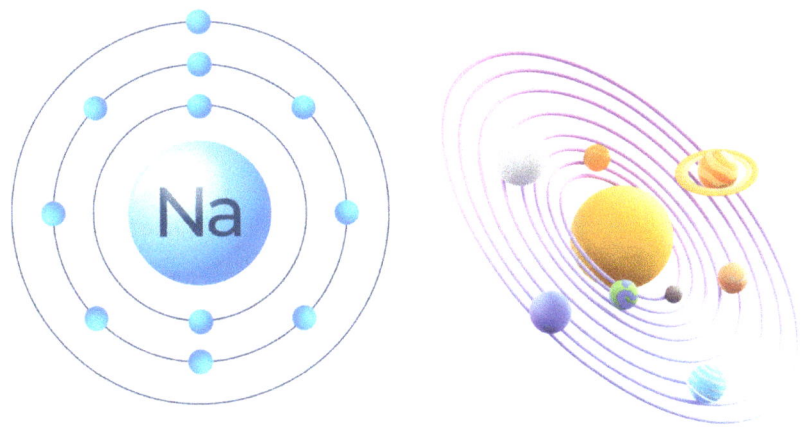

This principle also applies to human consciousness; the patterns we observe in our inner world reflect the patterns of the outer world. If chaos dominates the external world, it is because chaos dominates the minds of individuals. When we bring order, balance, and clarity to our personal consciousness, we begin to see these same qualities manifest in our external reality.

"The ancient Hermetists considered this Principle as one of the most important mental instruments by which man was able to pry aside the obstacles which hid from view the Unknown."

– The Kybalion.

III

THE PRINCIPLE OF VIBRATION

"Nothing Rests; Everything Moves"

"This Principle embodies the truth that "everything is in motion"; "everything vibrates"; "nothing is at rest"; facts which Modern Science endorses, and which each new scientific discovery tends to verify. And yet this Hermetic Principle was enunciated thousands of years ago, by the Masters of Ancient Egypt."

– The Kybalion.

If everything is in motion, then even objects that appear to be solid (rocks, metal, or human bodies) are composed of vibrating energy. The difference between matter and energy is simply the frequency at which they vibrate.

"This Principle explains that the differences between different manifestations of Matter, Energy, Mind, and even Spirit, result largely from varying rates of Vibration."

– The Kybalion.

Ice, water, and steam are all the same substance (H_2O), but their state of being depends on their vibrational frequency. When water (liquid) molecules slow down, they freeze into ice (solid). When they speed up, they become steam (gas).

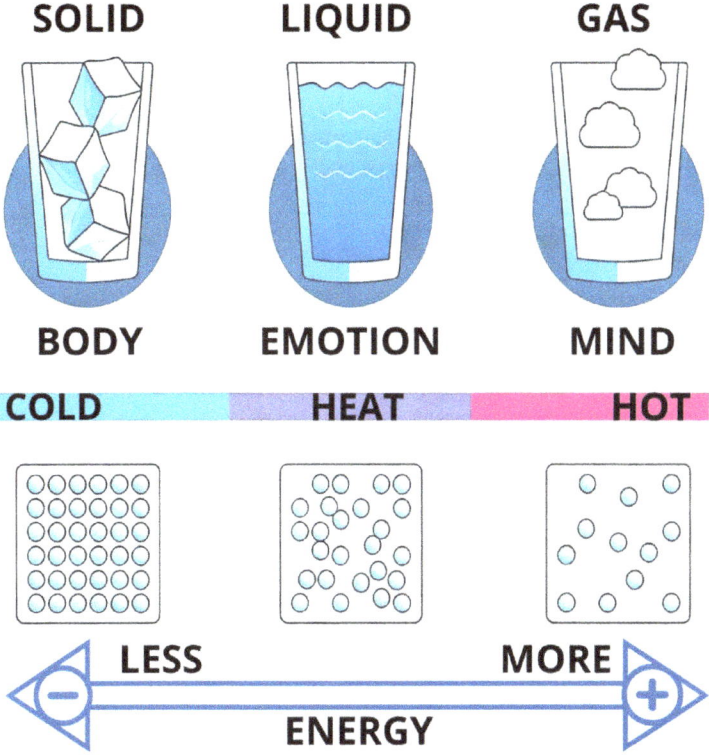

Similarly, our consciousness expresses in three core states of vibration: the body (solid), the sensations and emotions (liquid), and the mind (gas).

This law teaches us that we can alter our reality by defining our state of vibration through breath, movement, thought, emotion, and intention.

"An understanding of this enables students to control their own mental vibrations as well as those of others. The Masters also apply this Principle to the conquering of Natural phenomena, in various ways. "He who understands the Principle of Vibration, has grasped the sceptre of power," says one of the old writers."

– The Kybalion.

IV

THE PRINCIPLE OF POLARITY

"Everything Has Its Opposite"

"Everything is Dual; everything has poles; everything has its pair of opposites; like and unlike are the same; opposites are identical in nature, but different in degree; extremes meet; all truths are but half-truths; all paradoxes may be reconciled."

– The Kybalion.

Everything exists in duality: light and dark, expansion and contraction, positive and negative, up and down, hot and cold. These opposites are not in conflict but in complementary balance.

Heat and cold are not different things, they are different variational states of the same thing: Temperature.

V

THE PRINCIPLE OF RHYTHM

"Everything Moves in Cycles"

"Everything flows, out and in; everything has its tides; all things rise and fall; the pendulum-swing manifests in everything; the measure of the swing to the right is the measure of the swing to the left; rhythm compensates."

– The Kybalion.

Life follows natural cycles of rise and fall, expansion and contraction. Everything moves according to a universal rhythm, from the changing of seasons to the rise and fall of civilizations. None of this is "good" nor "bad" in nature; success and failure, pleasure and pain, hope and despair are not an objective reality, but rather a subjective interpretation of experience.

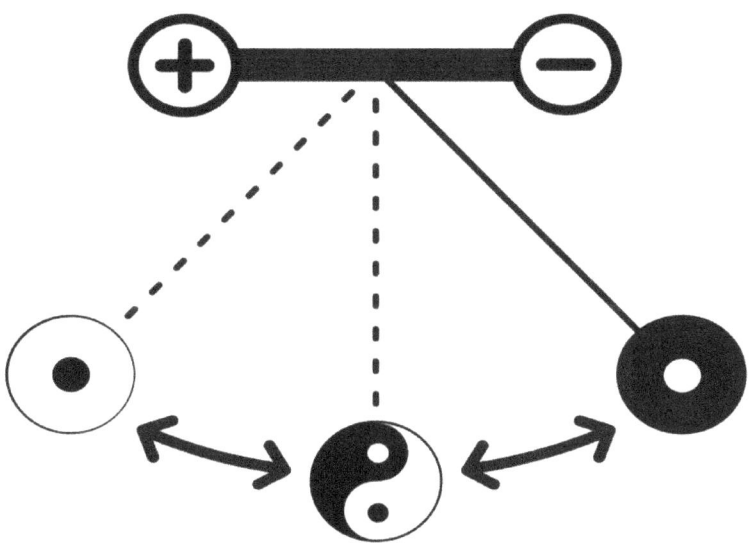

Understanding this rhythmic oscillation reveals one of the greatest keys to human resilience: **this too shall pass**. Every emotion, every high, every low is part of a broader pendulum swing of existence. And with that realization comes the power to transcend reactive living.

Each moment, whether joyful or painful, carries its own wisdom, its own alchemical seed of transformation. It offers a hidden opportunity to awaken beauty, to reveal meaning, and ultimately, to access **bliss** as a powerful and neutralized center between the extremes of perception.

The ancient Hermeticists referred to this capacity as: The **mental law of neutralization**, the inner art of consciously choosing the point of balance within the flux of opposites. When we master this principle, we activate what the mystics called mental alchemy: the ability to transmute any emotional or energetic state into a higher octave of experience. We rise above the swing of the pendulum not by stopping life's rhythms, but by learning how to ride them consciously, transmuting their energy through will, wisdom, and the tools of the Axis system.

VI

THE PRINCIPLE OF CAUSE AND EFFECT

"Every Action Has a Reaction"

"Every Cause has its Effect; every Effect has its Cause; everything happens according to Law; Chance is but a name for Law not recognized; there are many planes of causation, but nothing escapes the Law."

– The Kybalion.

There are no accidents. Everything happens because of something else. This principle teaches that nothing is random; our thoughts, words, and actions create ripples in the energetic field of consciousness, shaping our reality.

"The Hermetists understand the art and methods of rising above the ordinary plane of Cause and Effect… and by mentally rising to a higher plane they become Causers instead of Effects."

– The Kybalion.

If what is happening in your life does not arise from your conscious will, it is a clear sign: you must rise. You must elevate yourself to a new level of awareness, coherence, and power, so that you may become the cause of the effects you truly desire.

Yet even when you strive and succeed, even when you master your own field of cause and effect, you will never be beyond law itself. There will always be greater hierarchies of power, greater streams of influence, that shape existence at every scale; from the subatomic to the cosmic.

True mastery, therefore, is not the fantasy of lawlessness or separation, but the ability to align your will with the higher laws of consciousness and nature.

When your will is synchronized with higher cause, you radiate with power, integrity, and creative influence into the world.

VII

THE PRINCIPLE OF GENDER

"Everything Has Masculine and Feminine Forces"

"No creation, physical, mental or spiritual, is possible without this Principle. An understanding of its laws will throw light on many a subject that has perplexed the minds of men."

– The Kybalion.

This principle refers to the duality of creative forces in nature.

• Feminine Energy → Receptive, intuitive, magnetic. (Gravitational pull)

• Masculine Energy → Active, projective, electric. (Electrical radiation)

Creation requires both forces. When we integrate these energies within ourselves, we become balanced, whole, and fully capable of manifesting our highest potential.

"The Principle of Gender works ever in the direction of generation, regeneration, and creation. Everything, and every person, contains the two Elements or Principles, or this great Principle, within it, him or her.

Every Male thing has the Female Element also; every Female contains also the Male Principle."

– The Kybalion.

This Principle teaches us that although gender is visibly expressed as biological sex in all living forms, there is a far more subtle and profound manifestation of this law within us: the inner existence of the masculine and feminine principles. These two polarities do not simply pertain to physical form; they represent energetic qualities, currents of consciousness, present in all beings and in all levels of existence.

In the ancient yogic traditions, the feminine energetic current is known as Ida, while the masculine current is known as Pingala. These two energies weave themselves around the central channel of the human energy system, dancing in a continuous flow of exchange. Their movements converge at crucial points along the

spinal column, forming the seven core chakras: the vital energy centers of human consciousness.

This eternal weaving is beautifully symbolized by the Caduceus of Mercury, the ancient emblem depicting two serpents coiling around a central staff. Far from being a random symbol, the Caduceus encapsulates the profound truth of human nature, the tantric interplay of duality, and the secret of life itself. It is for this reason that the modern medical system adopted the Caduceus as its emblem;

because health is born from the harmonious weaving and balancing of these two inner forces.

The term Tantra, derived from Sanskrit, means "the science of weaving"; the sacred science of fusing opposites to create new possibilities. Tantra is not merely a spiritual discipline, but the very understanding of how the masculine and feminine forces are united to generate new life, new energy, and new dimensions of experience. Through the conscious mastery of these forces, one transcends binary perception and enters the vast creative freedom of neutrality, thereby elevating into higher realms of consciousness and experience.

Mastering the Principle of Gender is not about suppressing one polarity or favoring the other. It is the art of weaving them together, harmonizing action and receptivity, assertion and surrender, thought and feeling, into a living symphony of wholeness.

These are the seven Hermetic principles, they are beyond philosophy, these laws describe the actual energetic structure of the universe itself and AXIS is a system to understand how these laws apply to our human nature, the universe, and experience itself.

PART II

THE AXIS SYSTEM

CHAPTER V

AXIS SYSTEM
THE TRAINING OF CONSCIOUSNESS

THE INTEGRATION OF THE THREE FIELDS OF THE SELF

In the previous chapters, we explored the nature of consciousness as an electromagnetic toroidal field, where the interplay of magnetism (inward force, sensation) and electricity (outward force, action) forms the foundation of experience. Now, we will examine how this consciousness expresses itself through the three fields of the self:

1. The Physical Field (Foundation – Solid State):

• This is the structural and tangible aspect of being the material vessel that anchors experience into the physical world.

• It serves as the foundation upon which consciousness expresses itself in form.

2. The Emotional Field (Sensation – Liquid State):

• Emotions flow like water, shaping experience through movement, depth, and intensity.

• This field translates energy into feeling, coloring perception with emotional resonance.

3. The Mental Field (Perception – Gaseous State):

• The mind operates like air, expansive, intangible, and capable of shifting perspectives.

• It generates thoughts and interpretations, shaping the narrative we construct about our reality.

These three fields are not separate but different densities of the same electromagnetic force. Together, they create the engine of human experience, a dynamic interplay between consciousness, energy, and matter. The integration of these fields, with the fire at the core of the toroidal field, is the key to self-mastery. This inner fire is the "chi," the life force that allows us to transform, adapt, and manifest.

However, because consciousness operates within a sensorimotor spectrum, where sensations (magnetic) pull inward and actions (electric) radiate outward, we require a training system to regulate and harmonize these forces. This is where the Axis System comes into play.

A FRAMEWORK FOR HARMONIZING CONSCIOUSNESS

The Axis System was created to provide a structured method to balance and integrate the physical, emotional, and mental fields. By aligning these aspects, we optimize the function of our electromagnetic field, achieving greater coherence, clarity, and vitality.

At the core of this system is the understanding that magnetic force (sensation) and electric force (action) must be in equilibrium for optimal health and experience. An excess of inward pull without proper expression leads to stagnation, while excessive outward expression without adequate grounding leads to burnout. Balance is key.

Each field of the self has a corresponding training method within the Axis System:

1. Postural Training for the Physical Field (Structure & Stability)

Why? The body is the foundation of consciousness. A misaligned body leads to energy imbalances, tension, and inefficiency.

How? Practices like yoga asanas, Pilates, and postural exercises improve alignment, enhancing both physical and energetic flow.

• Scientific Backing: Research has shown that proper posture improves mood, self-confidence, and hormonal balance, reducing stress-related responses in the nervous system.

Physical training regulates sensory input, preventing overstimulation that leads to stress, fatigue, and injury.

2. Breathwork for the Emotional Field (Regulation & Flow)

Why? Breath is the bridge between body and mind. It regulates emotional states by controlling nervous system responses.

How? Practices like diaphragmatic breathing, pranayama, and structured breathwork help modulate emotional intensity, stabilize mood, and improve resilience.

• Scientific Backing: Controlled breathing techniques have been shown to reduce cortisol levels (stress hormone), improve emotional regulation, and enhance mental clarity.

Emotional mastery allows for fluidity in experience, preventing emotional stagnation or overwhelming surges.

3. Attention Training for the Mental Field (Focus & Perception)

Why? Where attention goes, energy flows. The ability to direct focus determines the quality of thought and the reality one creates.

How? Meditation, visualization, and structured focus exercises strengthen mental resilience and clarity.

• Scientific Backing: Studies in neuroscience confirm that focused attention rewires neural pathways, enhancing cognitive function and emotional stability.

Training the mind prevents overthinking, mental fragmentation, and unconscious reaction patterns, cultivating conscious perception.

By integrating these three training systems, we align the sensory (magnetic) and motor (electric) functions of consciousness, resulting in a harmonized, high-functioning human system. However, in the modern era, our engine is no longer running in harmony. With the acceleration of technology, overstimulation, and sedentary lifestyles, we have lost touch with the natural rhythms of regulation, leading to widespread mental and physical distress.

Let's apply this theory into the context of the two most common states of dysregulation: anxiety and depression. Let's understand how this principles of **Feeling** and **Acting** apply to each situation

ANXIETY:

OVERSTIMULATION WITHOUT PROPER OUTPUT

Anxiety occurs when too much input (sensation and feeling) floods the system without proper release. This results in overstimulation of the nervous system, causing:

• A hyperactive mental state (excessive thought loops, over-analysis).

• Physical symptoms (increased heart rate, shallow breathing, muscle tension).

• Emotional dysregulation (persistent worry, fear, or restlessness).

From an energetic perspective, this is an imbalance between magnetism (sensation) and electricity (action). Too much magnetic force without proper electric discharge leads to internal pressure and nervous system overload.

AXIS SOLUTION FOR ANXIETY:

• Postural training and active workout burn the extra energy and releases endocannabinoids that promote a chill and positive mood.

• Progressively slower and deeper breaths regulate the overstimulation of the nervous system, calming the talkative, compulsive mind.

• Attention training focuses energy, preventing chaotic thought loops.

DEPRESSION:

NUMBING AND ENERGY SUPPRESSION

Depression is the opposite imbalance to anxiety; where the system numbs itself due to trauma, stagnation, or depletion. Instead of too much fuel, the engine stalls, unable to generate enough combustion for motion. This manifests as:

• Apathy and lack of motivation (the mental field lacks the energy to create).

• Fatigue and heaviness (the body stops producing movement).

• Emotional shutdown (the fuel is suppressed, resulting in numbness).

Individuals experiencing depression often seek intense sensations (self-harm, substance abuse, extreme behaviors) to reignite their ability to feel. This is because the emotional field, when numbed, disconnects from the flow of experience, creating a void that demands stimulation.

AXIS SOLUTION FOR DEPRESSION:

• Postural training reactivates the body's capacity to engage with experience.

• Breathwork restores emotional connection and energetic balance.

• Attention training reintroduces mental engagement, breaking stagnation.

By expanding our energetic bandwidth and regulating sensory-motor balance, we prevent both burnout (from overdoing) and stagnation (from underdoing).

THE AXIS SYSTEM:

Now that we understand the problems of imbalance, we turn to the solution: The Axis System. This system provides a structured method for aligning the three fields of the self, ensuring that energy flows efficiently, experiences are processed effectively, and the engine of consciousness runs at full capacity.

In the following chapters, we will practically explore how to master each of these fields. Each chapter will provide techniques, exercises, and principles to integrate these aspects into daily life:

• Chapter 6: Mastering the Physical Field – The importance of postural alignment, movement, and body mechanics.

• Chapter 7: Mastering the Emotional Field – Harnessing breathwork to regulate emotions and expand vibrational capacity.

• Chapter 8: Mastering the Mental Field – Training attention and focus to shape reality through conscious perception.

• Chapter 9: Mastering the Energy Field – Energy as the Unifying Force – exploring how chi, spirit, and the core fire of creation integrate all three fields into one harmonious experience.

Through the Axis System, we learn not just to exist but to thrive; to transform our experience from unconscious reaction to conscious creation.

This is the path to the Self.

CHAPTER VI

MASTERING THE PHYSICAL FIELD

STRUCTURE & STABILITY

Gravity, Willpower, and the Axis of Posture.

The AXIS Postural System emerges from Hatha Raja Yoga science, where posture is understood as Asana. The most fundamental principle of Asana is simple but profound:

"Asana is a comfortable and stable posture."

-Sadguru

If your posture is not comfortable and stable, you are not in asana.

This principle comes from Hatha Yoga, a discipline that teaches us that:

• "Ha" means gravity (the downward pull, grounding force).

• "Tha" means willpower (the upward expansion, the drive of life).

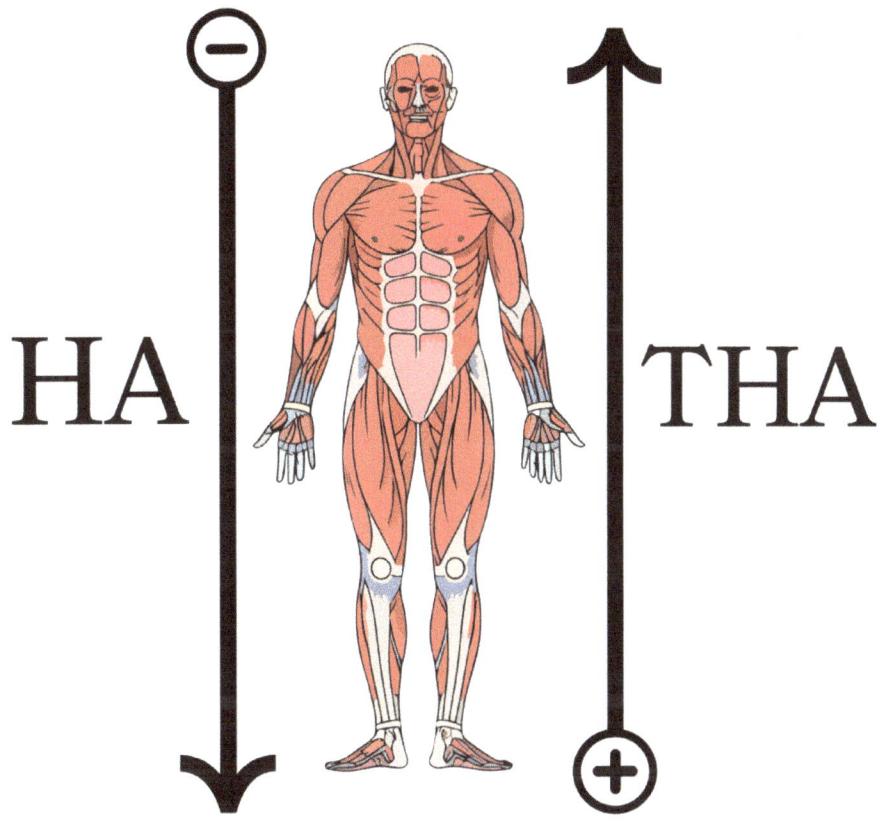

Hatha, therefore, represents the friction and relationship between gravity and willpower, between inertia and action, stability and movement, rest and awakening.

Just as the Hermetic Principles describe the duality of existence, we see this principle expressed within the body as:

• Gravity & Willpower

• Sleep & Wakefulness

• Life & Death

GRAVITY AND WILLPOWER AS LIFE & DEATH CYCLES

• Death as Gravity: When life leaves the body, it transitions from vertical (standing, alive) to horizontal (lying down, lifeless). Sleep follows the same principle; when we are falling asleep our gravitational force increases, our will power over our body decreases and the natural will of nature restores through the activation of the parasympathetic nervous system.

• Life as Willpower: During wakefulness, the willpower vector is dominant, keeping us upright, active, and engaged with our environment.

This cosmic duality operates within our physiology at all times, influencing our posture, metabolism, and energy flow.

In an aligned system, gravity and willpower work together; grounding us in stability while allowing for dynamic movement and expansion. But in a misaligned system, these forces are disrupted, leading to:

• Fatigue, tension, and imbalance

• Poor posture and misaligned energy flow

• Reduced vitality and inefficient movement

THE REAL CAUSE OF MODERN POSTURAL IMBALANCE

It's easy to blame screens, sedentarism, and lack of movement for the widespread postural dysfunction in modern society. While these factors contribute, they are symptoms rather than the root cause.

The deeper issue is that most people are out of sync with the natural cycles of energy, gravity, and willpower.

When we disconnect from the rhythms of nature, such as:

• Sunlight exposure (circadian regulation)

• Daily cycles of movement and rest

• Proper sleep-wake alignment

…we lose energy, become sedentary, and compensate with unnatural habits, leading to:

• Chronic fatigue and overstimulation

• Slouching, asymmetrical weight distribution, and weak posture

• A disconnection between body, breath, and attention

This is why posture is not merely a structural concern; it is the foundation upon which the body's biological, energetic, and psychological functions operate. The alignment of the body impacts metabolic efficiency, emotional regulation, and cognitive processing, making it one of the most fundamental yet overlooked aspects of human well-being.

While modern science has only recently begun to understand the profound effects of posture on health, ancient traditions have long recognized the body as an expression of sacred geometry; a precise and intentional design that reflects the underlying intelligence of nature.

The symmetry and proportion within the human form are not random; they align with principles found throughout the cosmos, suggesting that balance in the body is intrinsically connected to balance in life itself.

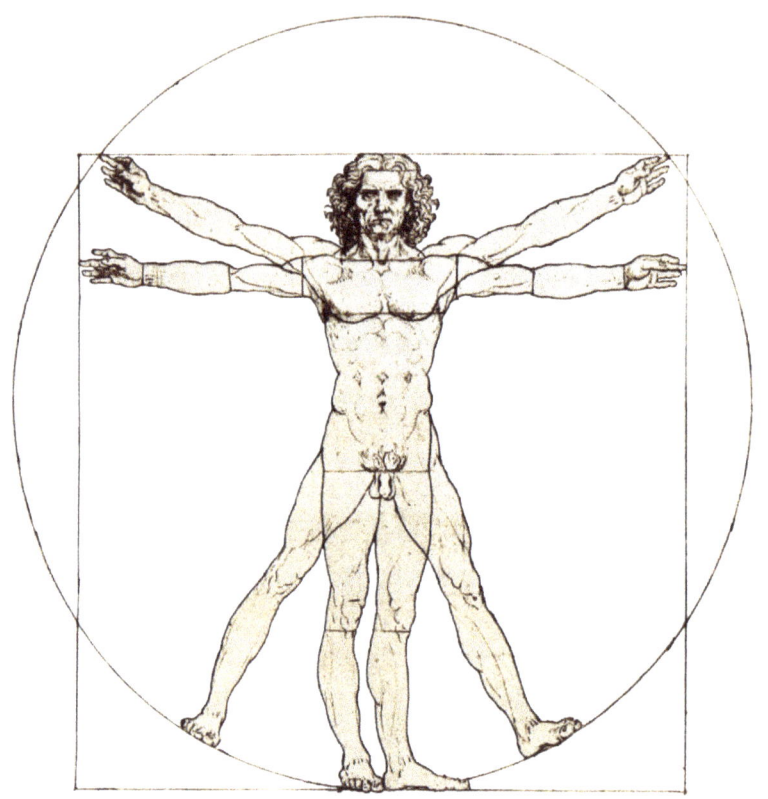

THE SCIENCE OF POSTURE AND METABOLIC EFFICIENCY

Scientific research has demonstrated that postural alignment plays a direct role in metabolic processes. When the body is aligned correctly, energy is distributed efficiently, allowing organs, muscles, and biological systems to function without unnecessary strain. A study published in BMC Public Health found that posture affects energy expenditure, with misalignments leading to inefficient use of muscle groups and increased metabolic cost (Cao et al., 2023). This suggests that maintaining optimal posture does not merely affect how we move, it influences how our bodies regulate energy at a fundamental level.

The benefits extend beyond energy conservation. Poor posture has been linked to compromised respiratory function, as slouched or misaligned positions reduce lung capacity and oxygen intake (Lee & Lee, 2019). This lack of oxygenation impacts cognitive clarity, cardiovascular health, and emotional stability, reinforcing the idea that correct alignment supports not just mechanical efficiency but systemic well-being.

Additionally, research suggests that spinal alignment influences digestion and gut function. The autonomic nervous system, which regulates digestion, is closely intertwined with spinal posture and movement. A misaligned spine can exert pressure on the Vagus nerve, which plays a key role in digestive regulation, potentially leading to issues such as poor nutrient absorption, sluggish metabolism, and increased stress response in the gut (Fornari et al., 2017).

SACRED GEOMETRY AND THE HUMAN BODY

Sacred geometry is the mathematical framework upon which nature organizes itself, from the spirals of galaxies to the proportions of DNA. This same geometric precision is present in the human form, reflecting the intelligence of biological design.

One of the most well-known ratios found in the human body is the Golden Ratio (1.618:1), also known as Phi. This ratio appears in the proportions of the face, the spacing of the joints, and the overall symmetry of the skeletal system. Studies on human anatomy confirm that proportions adhering to Phi are not just aesthetically pleasing but structurally sound, optimizing both movement efficiency and biomechanical stability (Livio, 2002).

Further evidence suggests that the structural symmetry of the body directly correlates with health outcomes. A study in The Journal of Anatomy found that individuals with higher bodily symmetry exhibit greater musculoskeletal efficiency, lower injury rates, and improved balance (Manning & Pickup, 1998).

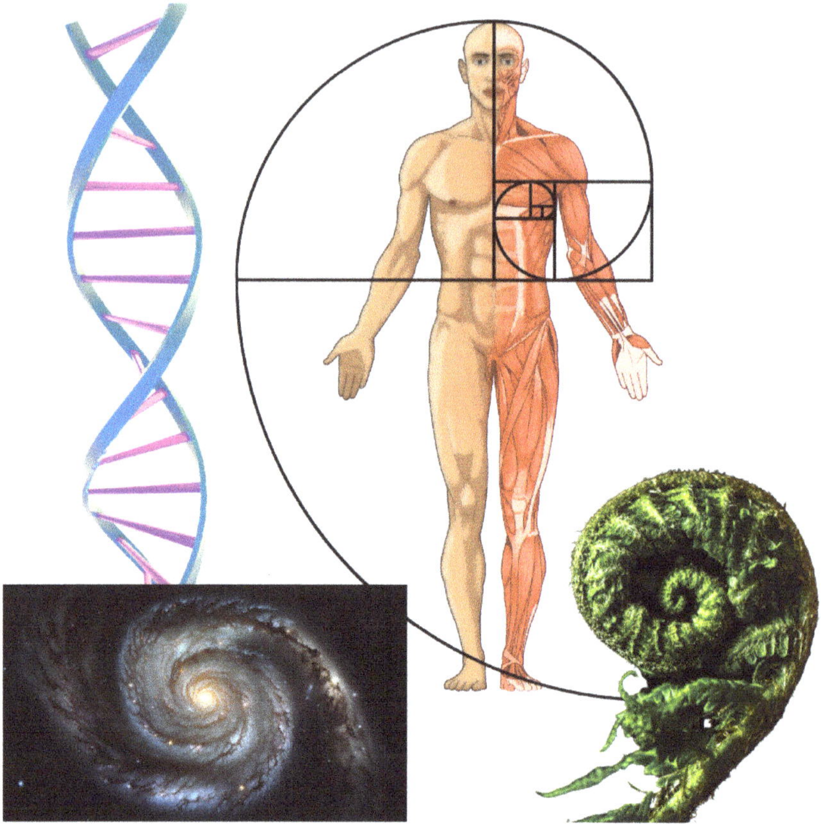

The Fibonacci sequence is a foundational aspect of sacred geometry, and is evident in the curvature of the spine, the branching of the nervous system, and even the rhythm of the heartbeat. The presence of these mathematical structures suggests that when the body is aligned according to its natural geometry, it operates in a state of coherence, reducing stress and enhancing vitality.

FIBONACCI SEQUENCE

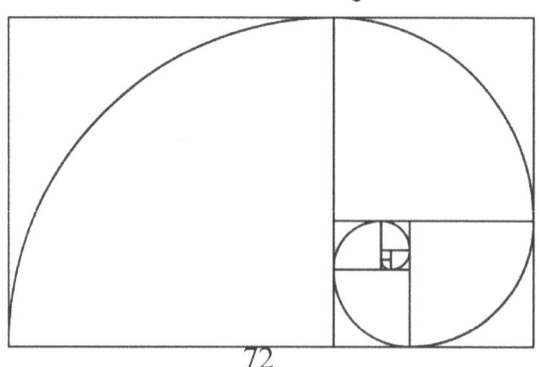

GOLDEN RATIO

$$\frac{a}{b} = \frac{a+b}{a} = 1.618....=\Phi$$

POSTURE, EMOTIONAL PROCESSING, AND MENTAL HEALTH.

Beyond its physiological effects, posture has a profound impact on emotional regulation and psychological health. Research has consistently demonstrated that body alignment influences cognitive processing, mood, and stress resilience.

One of the most striking findings in posture research is its relationship with stress response and self-perception. A study published in Health Psychology found that individuals who maintained an upright posture during stressful situations exhibited lower cortisol levels, greater emotional resilience, and higher confidence compared to those who slouched (Nair et al., 2015). This suggests that posture is not simply a response to emotion but a tool for actively shaping emotional states.

Further, studies in cognitive neuroscience have identified a direct link between posture and emotional recall. A paper in Cognition & Emotion demonstrated that participants who sat upright were more likely to access positive memories, while those who slouched were more prone to negative recollections (Riskind & Gotay, 1982). This reinforces the idea that posture acts as a physical anchor for psychological patterns, meaning that maintaining alignment may serve as a form of subtle but effective emotional regulation.

Additionally, posture influences social perception and personal agency. Researchers in the field of embodied cognition have found that expansive, open postures increase testosterone levels and

73

reduce stress hormones, leading to greater self-assurance and assertiveness (Carney et al., 2010). These findings align with ancient yogic teachings that emphasize the power of body positioning (Asanas) in cultivating inner strength and confidence.

POSTURE AS THE AXIS OF WELL-BEING

Posture is not merely a mechanical function; it is a structural key that influences energy distribution, metabolic efficiency, psychological resilience, and emotional processing. The alignment of the human body adheres to precise geometric patterns, reinforcing the idea that harmony in structure leads to harmony in function.

Scientific research has now validated what ancient traditions have long understood: the body is not just a physical entity but an energetic and structural masterpiece, designed for balance, efficiency, and expansion.

By mastering posture, we are not simply adjusting our external appearance, we are activating a deeper intelligence within the body, unlocking its highest potential for health, clarity, and power.

AXIS POSTURAL SOLUTION

Since most of us cannot simply abandon our societal commitments to return to a fully nature-synced lifestyle, the AXIS System offers a way to counterbalance this misalignment.

This is where conscious proprioception comes into play, because when we use posture as the structure of our experience, we can:

• Prevent injuries and chronic misalignment.

• Optimize the body's energy efficiency.

• Enhance metabolic and endocrine function.

• Align gravity (grounding) and willpower (expansion) to enhance presence and power.

AXIS POSTURAL EXERCISE:

ALIGNING THE VECTORS OF GRAVITY

Now, let's bring this into practice with an extra simple, one-minute alignment exercise that you can do anywhere, anytime. Don't mistake the simplicity of this exercise, aligning the weight distribution is the core and most important step in aligning with the Axis, with your power, with yourself. Use all the time you need.

This practice is rooted in proprioception, also known as the sixth sense: the ability to feel and adjust the internal structure of your body in space.

By consciously aligning your weight, structure, and energy, you reclaim sovereignty over your posture, movement, and experience.

Step 1: Becoming Aware of Your Contact Points

• If you are standing, feel the soles of your feet connecting to the ground.

• If you are sitting, feel the chair supporting you and the contact points between your body and the surface.

• Notice how your weight is distributed.

Step 2: Finding Left-Right Balance

• Without changing anything, observe: Is there more weight on your left or right side?

• Most of the time, we unconsciously favor one hemisphere, creating imbalances in posture.

• Gently shift the weight to the opposite side, then return to center, balancing your axis equally between left and right.

Step 3: Finding Front-Back Balance

• Now, observe: Is your weight more toward the front of your feet/body or the back?

• Many people unknowingly lean forward or backward, influencing their nervous system and emotional state.

• Gently shift the weight in the opposite direction, then find a neutral center.

Step 4: Aligning the Vertical Axis

• Feel the connection between your feet and the top of your head.

• Engage your core lightly and feel your spine elongating as if being pulled upward from the crown.

• Your knees should be activated but not locked, allowing for subtle micro-adjustments.

• Your hips, ribs, shoulders, and jaw should all be aligned along the central axis.

Step 5: Expanding the Energy Field

• Now that your gravity vectors are balanced, expand your presence:

• Root yourself deep into the earth (gravity, grounding).

• Expand your head and upper body upward (willpower, expansion).

• Allow your breath to move freely through this aligned axis

Make sure that your weight (which is the blueprint of your energies) is centered and your hemispheres balanced, so that your power is concentrated.

Practice this exercise every-day when you stand up from bed and step into the world!

This exercise balances and centers the structure of our life force, and is the base of a more complex and mystical exploration.

THE MYSTICISM OF POSTURE

Posture isn't just mechanical alignment, it is the support for the electromagnetic structure that transmits consciousness.

• In yoga and Kabbalah, an aligned posture allows for a clear transmission of consciousness through the central energy channel.

• In physics, a symmetrical system is more energy-efficient, allowing for greater power with less effort.

• In somatic studies, proper posture optimizes nervous system function, reducing stress and improving vitality.

When the spine is aligned, the body's transmission of energy is optimized, allowing for greater clarity, power, and presence.

By practicing this one-minute realignment daily, you'll prevent energy drainage, enhance mental clarity and emotional balance by regulating energy distribution, and improve breathing, circulation, and nervous system regulation.

This is the first step toward self-mastery: aligning your physical axis so that your energy flows effortlessly.

EXPANDING BEYOND THE PHYSICAL

Now that we've aligned the physical structure, we move into the emotional and mental dimensions.

In the next chapter, we will explore:

- The Breath as the Bridge Between Body and Mind
- How Breathwork Regulates Emotional Energy
- Techniques for Nervous System Regulation

By integrating posture (structure) and breath (flow), we unlock the next level of mastery: The ability to control our emotional state with precision.

CHAPTER VII

MASTERING THE EMOTIONAL FIELD

REGULATION & FLOW

In the previous chapter, we explored how posture and gravity regulate the body's energy flow. Now, we enter the deeper science of Yoga: the science of Pranayama, the practice of mastering the flow of energy through breath.

प्राणायाम

THE ART OF PRANAYAMA

The Breath as the Bridge Between Matter and Consciousness

The word Pranayama (प्राणायाम) comes from Sanskrit and is composed of:

- Prana (प्राण) → Meaning life force, energy, or breath (also known as Ki, Qi, or Chi).

- Yama (यम) → Meaning care, control, or regulation.

However, there is another interpretation:

- Ayama (आयाम) → Meaning expansion or extension.

Thus, Pranayama can be understood as both the regulation and expansion of energy.

In essence, Pranayama is the science of feeling.

- Posture (Asana) is about being.

- Breath (Pranayama) is about feeling.

- Thought (Dhyana) is about perceiving.

Even further, Pranayama relates to two simultaneous actions:

- To carry the energy; meaning to direct it, move it, and distribute it.
- To care for the energy; meaning to hold, preserve, and balance it.

This means that breath is not just air; it is not just the processing of oxygen. Breath is the fundamental vehicle of consciousness, regulating our energy, emotions, and mental state by determining where the energy is moving towards and regulating the amount of energy that is being processed throughout the system.

THE SCIENCE OF BREATH: BRIDGING MIND AND BODY.

Breath is the subtle thread that weaves together the tapestry of our physical and mental states. It serves as both a mirror reflecting our current condition and a tool capable of transforming it. Modern scientific research has begun to uncover the profound impact of breathwork on health, emotional regulation, and cognitive function. More than just a physiological necessity, breath is the gateway to self-mastery; a direct link between the body, the mind, and consciousness itself.

The autonomic nervous system (ANS), which governs involuntary bodily functions, is divided into the sympathetic (fight-or-flight) and parasympathetic (rest-and-digest) branches. Breath is unique in that it operates under both conscious and unconscious control, allowing us to influence the ANS deliberately. Slow, deep breathing techniques have been shown to activate the parasympathetic nervous system, promoting relaxation, focus, and emotional balance (Zaccaro et al., 2018).

A meta-analysis published in Scientific Reports concluded that breathwork is effective in improving stress and mental health, affirming that deliberate breath control is a powerful biohacking tool for self-regulation (Zaccaro et al., 2022).

The Physiological Sigh:

A Tool for Immediate Stress Reduction

Neuroscientist Dr. Andrew Huberman has highlighted the efficacy of a specific breathing technique known as the "physiological sigh", a method for rapid stress reduction. This technique involves two consecutive inhales through the nose, followed by an extended exhale through the mouth.

• The first inhale inflates the lungs partially, and the second inhale ensures that alveoli (tiny air sacs in the lungs) fully expand.

• The extended exhale allows for maximum expulsion of carbon dioxide, reducing physiological stress and inducing relaxation.

Huberman notes that even brief, structured breathwork protocols can positively impact mood, increase focus, improve physical endurance, and enhance sleep (Huberman, 2021).

This scientifically supported technique is one of the most accessible and immediate ways to shift one's state from anxious or reactive to calm and focused.

BREATHWORK AND EMOTIONAL REGULATION

Controlled breathing exercises are directly linked to emotional regulation. Breath is the primary modulator of the Vagus nerve, which governs emotional response, resilience, and relaxation. A study published in Frontiers in Psychology found that slow-paced breathing enhances emotional control, reinforcing the idea that breath can override impulsive emotional reactions and promote a measured, composed state of mind (Zaccaro et al., 2022).

This suggests that breathwork is not just a relaxation tool, but a fundamental practice for developing emotional intelligence.

Breath serves as the space between impulse and response, the bridge between thought and action. It is the first step in conscious regulation, allowing individuals to create a pause between external stimuli and internal reaction. This aligns with research showing that breathwork can enhance mood, reduce physiological arousal, and sharpen cognitive function, allowing for more deliberate, focused, and intentional decision-making (Balban et al., 2023).

In essence, by controlling our breath, we gain mastery over our reactions, thoughts, and energy output.

INTEGRATING BREATHWORK INTO DAILY LIFE

Breathwork is one of the most accessible, effective, and scientifically supported methods for optimizing physical, emotional, and cognitive performance. Unlike other self-regulation practices, it requires no special tools, locations, or equipment; only awareness and practice.

Some of the simplest and most effective breathwork techniques include:

• Diaphragmatic breathing (deep belly breathing) for relaxation and grounding.

• Box breathing (equal-length inhale, hold, exhale, hold) for focus and stability.

• Physiological sighs for immediate stress relief.

• Cyclic hyperventilation (Wim Hof Method) for increased oxygenation and energy.

As research continues to reveal the deep connections between breath, body, and mind, it is clear that conscious breathwork is one of the most powerful, natural, and scientifically backed tools for achieving balance, resilience, and expanded awareness.

Breath is the silent force regulating our experience of life. It influences heart rate, emotional state, cognitive clarity, and overall well-being.

It is the first thing we do upon arrival into this world, and the last thing we do before departing. It is the force that bridges body and mind, thought and action, being and becoming.

INTRODUCTION TO BREATHWORK PRACTICES

Now that we have explored the science and power of breath, it is time to move from theory to practice. Breathwork is not just an intellectual concept, it is an embodied experience, a tool to be actively engaged with.

The following four exercises are designed to target different aspects of breath control, allowing you to:

• Regulate emotional states and shift between relaxation, focus, and energy.

• Enhance mental clarity by optimizing oxygen intake and reducing physiological stress.

• Strengthen your nervous system to build resilience against external pressures.

Each of these techniques serves a unique purpose, from grounding and relaxation to stimulating clarity and focus. These practices are not meant to be rigid or dogmatic.

Experiment with them, observe how your body responds, and integrate the ones that serve you best.

As with all practices in the Axis System, breath is a personal journey. It is about learning to listen to your own rhythms, understanding how your breath influences your thoughts and emotions, and ultimately reclaiming mastery over your internal state.

Let's begin.

PRACTICAL BREATHWORK EXERCISES
FOR EMOTIONAL REGULATION

The following exercises will guide you through different frequencies of breath, allowing you to control your emotional states and energy levels.

Exercise 1:

4-4-4-4 Balanced Breath

Purpose: This breath pattern creates equilibrium between inhalation, retention, exhalation, and emptiness, stabilizing emotions and balancing the nervous system.

Steps:

1. Inhale (Puraka) for 4 counts – Slowly draw the breath in through the nose, feeling the expansion in your diaphragm.

2. Hold (Kumbhaka) for 4 counts – Maintain the inhalation, feeling the energy circulate.

3. Exhale (Rechaka) for 4 counts – Slowly release through the nose, allowing tension to melt away.

4. Hold empty (Shunyaka) for 4 counts – Remain still and grounded before beginning the next cycle.

Practice this for 5-10 minutes to cultivate emotional balance and energetic stability.

Exercise 2:

Expanding Breath Capacity (6-8-12 Method)

Purpose: Expanding the breath's length lowers its frequency, activating deeper states of relaxation and grounding the lower chakras.

Steps:

1. Begin with 6-count inhale, 6-count exhale, 4-count retention.

2. Expand to 8-count inhale, 8-count exhale, 4-count retention.

3. Progress to 12-count inhale, 12-count exhale, 4-count retention.

4. Continue increasing retention time to 6, 8, 10, and eventually 12 counts.

This exercise enhances lung capacity, strengthens the nervous system, and deepens emotional processing.

Exercise 3:

Breath of Fire (Kapalabhati)

This rapid, rhythmic breathing increases frequency, stimulating upper chakras and mental clarity. The word Kapalabhati comes from Kapala (कपाल) which means skull and Bhati which means to brilliant, or to polish (भाति), so try it out and feel how it burn all the thought away by the intensity of its emotion.

Steps:

1. Establish the Core Point (Manipura)

Bring awareness to Manipura, about 2-3 inches above and inside the navel. This is the diaphragm center, from which the breath will be pumped.

2. Axial Inhalation

Inhale deeply while elongating the spine. Create space between every vertebra, expanding upward through the crown and downward through the pelvis, widening the space between ribcage and hips. The axis is centered and vertical.

3. Active Exhalation

Exhale sharply by drawing Manipura up and in / up and back, pumping the diaphragm toward the heart and lungs. The contraction is quick, precise, and rhythmic.

4. Passive Inhalation

Allow the inhalation to happen naturally as the abdomen releases. Do not pull air in; the inhale is a rebound, created by the exhale.

5. Rhythm & Duration

Focus on steady rhythm, not counting.

• Beginners: slower, even pulses.

• Advanced: shorter, stronger exhalations with increased intensity.

Practice 5–30 seconds, up to 60 seconds maximum. Do not exceed this to avoid overloading the nervous system.

Exercise 4:

The Full Spectrum of Breath Frequency

Purpose: Understanding breath as a wavelength: longer breath-waves activate lower chakras, while shorter breathwaves activate higher chakras.

Steps:

1. Begin with slow, deep breaths (low frequency, wide waves). Activates Muladhara, Swadhisthana, and Manipura.

2. Gradually shorten the breath cycles while increasing frequency. Stimulates Anahata, Vishuddha, and Ajna.

3. Eventually, shift into Breath of Fire (extremely short, high-frequency breaths). Fully activates Sahasrara.

This exercise teaches you how to modulate your state of being through controlled breath rhythms.

AXIS BREATH

Axis Inhalation: begins at Manipura, the core center just above the navel. From this point, the inhalation expands simultaneously downward and upward, creating space between every vertebra. The expansion continues beyond the sacrum into the legs and beyond the crown into space, opening not only the spine but also the internal tissues and energetic circuitry. This expansion supports the activation and enlargement of the vital field.

Axis Exhalation: is always centered. During the exhale, the entire energetic field is gently gathered toward the central vertical axis — the spine, extended through the legs and the skull. As the field is drawn inward, it is naturally expressed through the poles: the crown and the soles of the feet. This action increases the coherence and magnitude of the electromagnetic field, which functions as a toroidal system. The exhalation is therefore a process of centering, elongating, and polarizing energy.

Axis Retentions: whether after inhalation or exhalation, are not performed by closing the valves of the breath. Instead, the glottis remains open, and the retention is created simply by pausing the movement of the diaphragm. In this state, breath flow is suspended without blocking circulation, allowing a subtle exchange between inner and outer fields. This in-between space — neither inhalation nor exhalation — is the mystic interval, where perception, vibration, and proprioception can shift in profound ways.

These practices are not meant to be isolated techniques performed once and forgotten, but training moments to understand the full range of breath and its capacity to activate different emotional, perceptual, and energetic states through variations in depth, rhythm, frequency, and retention.

MASTERING THE SPECTRUM OF FEELING AND EMOTION

When you master breath, you master emotion.

When you master emotion, you master energy flow.

And as you progressively master energy flow, you gain more control over your reactions and perceptions.

CHAPTER VIII
MASTERING THE MENTAL FIELD

PERCEPTION & NARRATIVE

The mind is often described as a mystery, a tool, a burden, or a gift, depending on who is speaking about it. But one of the most powerful explanations of the mind came to me in Sibundoy, Putumayo, Colombia, before an ayahuasca ceremony, when a shaman master asked me a simple yet profound question:

"What is the mind?"

I gave him an answer that felt complex and intellectual:

"The mind is the perceptual consequence of sensorial stimuli."

He laughed and shook his head.

"Too complicated," he said.

Then he told me:

"The mind is the narrative you have of yourself and the world you live in; the story you tell yourself."

And that changed everything!

This is the key to mastering the mental field: realizing that the mind is a storyteller. It is constantly weaving a narrative about who we are, what we can or cannot do, and how the world works.

This inner dialogue can be a source of empowerment or a source of self-sabotage. It can lift us up, give us strength, and guide us toward our highest ideals, or it can hold us back, filling us with doubt, fear, and limitation.

To master the mental field is to master this inner dialogue, to shape our thoughts and perception in a way that aligns with clarity, power, and truth.

THE GREAT MISUNDERSTANDING

"I Think, Therefore I Am"

One of the greatest misconceptions about the mind comes from René Descartes, who famously said:

"Cogito, ergo sum." (I think, therefore I am.)

This phrase has shaped Western thought, reinforcing the idea that thinking is the essence of existence. But is this true?

No.

Thinking is one expression of cognition, but it is not the only expression of mental activity. Mystics, yogis, shamans, and masters of consciousness have shown for thousands of years that thought is only one aspect of mind.

The truth is that we ARE, therefore, we BREATHE, therefore we FEEL, therefore we THINK, therefore we MOVE, therefore we HAVE.

This is the order and hierarchy of existence, the path from being to having. Descartes was wrong in the sense that Thinking is not the source of human existence. Breath is what sustains our life, then sensation input (feeling) takes in the building blocks of information that the mind organizes and signifies through the thinking process, enabling one to act consciously; and therefore, to HAVE. Have what? THE INTEGRATED HUMAN EXPERIENCE

If we think before we ARE, if we think before we BREATHE, if we think before we FEEL, we alter the order of experience and start overthinking things that are not meant to be thought. We are not meant to overthink our exitance, our breath and our feelings, these are dimensions to our existence that require no active thoughts to be performed and are in fact, the source of thought (not the other way around).

The integrated Human experience is the result of understanding that life's Axis lies in the capacity of the body to BE, BREATHE, FEEL and MOVE. The thinking process and the experience is the result of the interaction between all these dimensions of our existence.

To train the mind, we must learn to guide our attention beyond thinking. This is the only way we can enter states of deep focus, meditation, and stillness, where the mind becomes a tool for experience, instead of the master of experience.

TRAINING THE MIND

The Three Stages of Meditation

In Patanjali's Yoga Sutras, meditation is described as a three-step process, which forms part of the Eight Limbs of Yoga:

1.   Dharana (धारणा) - "Certainty" – To Decide.

2.   Dhyana (ध्यान) - "Meditation" – To Concentrate.

3.   Samadhi (समाधि) - "Absorption" – To Become.

These three stages mirror the process of mastering perception and narrative. Let's explore them in depth.

धारणा

Dharana

The Power of Attention

Dharana means "concentration" or "one-pointed focus." It is the practice of holding the mind steady on a single object of awareness.

How Dharana Works:

- The mind, which is usually scattered and jumping between thoughts, is deliberately anchored to one point.
- This could be the breath, a mantra, a candle flame, a visualization, or an idea.
- Dharana is the decision to focus; the first step in rewriting your narrative.

Practice:

- Trataka (त्राटक) → Staring at a candle flame without distraction.
- Japa (जप) → Repeating a mantra like "Om" or "So Hum."
- Anapana Sati → Observing the breath without reacting.

Dharana is like setting the camera lens of your perception; choosing what to focus on.

ध्यान

Dhyana

The Flow of Awareness

Dhyana is meditation, the active practice of consciously directing the flow of attention.

How Dhyana Works:

- The mind stops "trying" to concentrate, it simply rests in awareness.
- Thoughts fade into the background, but you are still aware.
- The observer (you) and the object of meditation merge into one process.

Practice:

- Becoming fully absorbed in the rhythm of your breath.
- Feeling one with nature, as if there is no separation between you and the world.
- Meditating on pure stillness, where thoughts arise but do not disturb.

Dhyana is like entering "the flow state", that moment when one trains and creates in the flow of action; a runner lost in movement, a musician lost in sound, an actor lost in a role.

समाधि

Samadhi

The Dissolution of Self

Samadhi is complete absorption into consciousness itself.

How Samadhi Works:

- The sense of individuality dissolves, you no longer feel separate from what you are meditating on.
- The mind ceases to fluctuate, there is only presence, only awareness, only existence itself.
- Time disappears, space disappears, there is only the experience of being.

Example of Samadhi Experience:

- Becoming so deeply absorbed in meditation that you lose awareness of the body.
- The moments of intense orgasm where the idea of "you" disappears by the magnitude of the sensations.
- A feeling of infinite connection, oneness, and stillness beyond words.

Samadhi is merging into your desired subject, object or point of attention.

When achieve Samadhi you are no longer a drop of water in the ocean, you are the ocean in a drop of water. You are no longer your identity, you become free to access the magic of your nature as human, consciousness and life force.

THE SCIENCE OF ATTENTION AND
THE CONSTRUCTION OF THE SELF

Attention is the fundamental force shaping our perception, memory, and ultimately, our self-narrative. Every moment of awareness is like a frame in a film reel, constructing the story of our lives in real-time.

The ability to direct and sustain attention is not a passive trait, but an active skill that can be developed and refined. Just as a filmmaker selects which shots to include in a movie, our attention selects which moments define us, influencing how we interpret events, how we emotionally process experiences, and how we create our sense of self.

In this way, attention is not just an input system, it is a means through which we develop and define of identity, our self-narrative.

ATTENTION AS THE ARCHITECT OF EXPERIENCE

The human brain does not record reality as an objective stream of data; instead, it selectively filters and encodes information based on what we pay attention to. This means that our experience of the world is not just about what happens, but about what we notice, what we recall, and how we frame those events within our internal narrative.

Neuroscientist Michael Posner, one of the leading researchers on attention, describes it as "the mechanism that selects and amplifies information, shaping what enters conscious awareness" (Posner & Petersen, 1990). Studies have confirmed that attention acts as a gatekeeper to perception, filtering out irrelevant stimuli and reinforcing patterns of thought and behavior based on repeated focus.

A study on episodic memory consolidation found that attention plays a decisive role in shaping long-term memory by amplifying emotionally salient moments (Schacter, Addis, & Buckner, 2007). This means that the more we focus on a particular thought, feeling, or event, the more deeply it imprints into our identity (This is a concept echoed in both neuroscience and Jungian psychology).

Carl Jung explored this process through his concept of individuation, which suggests that attention to inner thought patterns allows us to integrate unconscious aspects of the self into conscious awareness (Jung, 1959). In other words, becoming aware of our attention patterns allows us to shape our personal evolution, choosing which aspects of the self to reinforce and which to deconstruct.

ATTENTION AND SELF-NARRATIVE

Every moment of focused attention functions as a narrative point, a photogram in the film of our personal story. Over time, these points become the defining structure of our self-concept.

For example, two people might experience the same event but focus on entirely different aspects, creating two completely different memories and emotional responses. One person might attend to the challenge and growth that came from it, while another might focus on the frustration or fear it caused. Their attention determines what story they tell themselves about the experience, which in turn influences their future behavior and expectations.

Cognitive science supports this idea, showing that repeated attention to certain thoughts strengthens neural pathways, making those thought patterns more likely to become habitual and automatic (Hebb, 1949). This aligns with Dr. Joe Dispenza's assertion that "neurons that fire together, wire together". Meaning that: where we place our attention repeatedly, we create a reinforced narrative that influences our entire perception of reality (Dispenza, 2014).

Furthermore, research in cognitive psychology has demonstrated that attention shapes not only memory but also emotional processing. A study by Riskind & Gotay (1982) found that people who adopted an upright posture and directed their attention toward positive memories were more likely to access additional positive memories, while those who focused on negative experiences had increased difficulty recalling positive ones. This demonstrates how attention is directly linked to our emotional state and overall worldview.

MEDITATION: TRAINING ATTENTION

If attention is the force shaping experience, then the ability to control and direct attention is one of the most powerful skills a person can develop. Meditation is one of the most well-documented methods for doing exactly that.

Studies have shown that Focused Attention Meditation (FAM) enhances the ability to sustain focus, reduce mind-wandering, and increase cognitive flexibility. A meta-analysis on meditation and attention found that long-term meditation practitioners exhibited increased activation in the anterior cingulate cortex, a brain region associated with attention control (Tang, Hölzel, & Posner, 2015).

Dr. Amishi Jha's research on mindfulness-based attention training demonstrates that regular meditation practice significantly enhances sustained attention and working memory, particularly in high-stress environments such as military training and elite sports (Jha, Morrison, Parker, & Stanley, 2020). This suggests that attention can be trained just as any muscle can be strengthened through deliberate practice.

Additionally, a study by Brewer et al. (2011) found that meditation reduces activity in the default mode network (DMN), the brain region responsible for self-referential thoughts and mind-wandering. By quieting the DMN, meditation allows individuals to focus more fully on the present moment, reducing negative rumination and unconscious mental loops.

This aligns with Jung's concept of individuation, as well as Dispenza's assertion that "by directing attention away from habitual thought patterns, we create the space to rewire our perception of reality" (Dispenza, 2014).

Beyond its impact on self-narrative, attention training has been extensively studied for its broader cognitive and emotional benefits:

> • Mindfulness training improves attentional performance in high-stress professionals, reinforcing the idea that meditation enhances focus and cognitive resilience (Jha et al., 2020).

> • Long-term meditation practitioners exhibit increased gray matter density in brain regions associated with self-awareness, emotional regulation, and cognitive flexibility, suggesting that attention training physically alters the brain to support higher-order thinking (Lazar et al., 2005).

> • A meta-analysis of meditation studies found that regular practice reduces symptoms of depression, anxiety, and emotional reactivity, providing evidence that attention training influences not only cognition but deep-seated emotional responses (Goyal et al., 2014).

EXERCISE

TRAINING THE POWER OF ATTENTION

1. Choose one thing you want to bring more into your life.

    - This could be a word, phrase, concept, or goal.
    - Example: "The future is bright."

2. Create a sigil or symbol using the initials of the phrase.

    - Example: T F I B → merge these letters into a symbol.

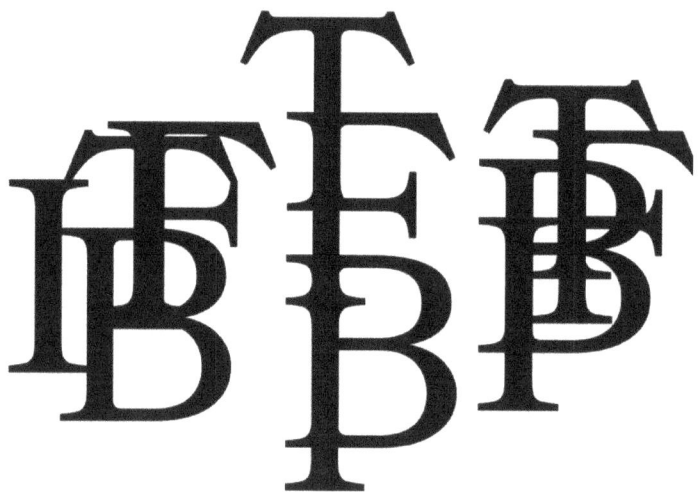

3. Place your attention on it for a specific amount of time.

    - Start with 3 minutes.
    - If comfortable, increase to 5, 7, or 10 minutes.

4. Breathe with the sigil.

    - Inhale → Think the phrase.
    - Exhale → Say it silently or aloud.

5.   Apply this exercise to increment your presence and awareness into all kinds of daily actions.

- Meditate while working, walking, or interacting with others.
- Let presence become part of your everyday life.

The goal is not just to meditate with eyes closed, but to meditate in action, to bring awareness into every moment.

By training Dharana, Dhyana, and Samadhi, and by choosing where to direct your perception, you are actively writing your own narrative instead of passively reacting to life.

Attention is the foundation of conscious experience. It determines what we focus on, how we interpret reality, and ultimately, how we construct our sense of self. Attention is not just a passive function; it is the active force that writes the script of our personal narrative.

Through meditation and mindfulness practices, we train ourselves to direct this force consciously, choosing which thoughts to reinforce, which emotions to engage with, and which aspects of reality to focus on. Neuroscience confirms that the ability to control attention directly shapes perception, memory, and emotional well-being.

By understanding attention as the primary architect of self-narrative, we unlock the ability to consciously shape our lives, rather than being shaped by unconscious thought patterns.

Your attention is your lens. Your perception is your movie.

Every moment is a photogram. The story is yours to tell.

CHAPTER IX
MASTERING THE ENERGY FIELD
The Unification of the Self.

THE ENERGY FIELD: THE UNIFYING FORCE OF EXISTENCE

The energy field is not separate from the physical, emotional, and mental fields; it is the unified force that contains them all. It is the source from which they emerge and the medium through which they interact.

It is crucial to understand that these fields are not different entities, but different densities of the same field:

• The physical field is the densest expression of energy, manifesting as the body, posture, and structure.

• The emotional field is the fluid expression of energy, shaping our experience of movement, sensation, and vibrational states.

• The mental field is the lightest and most expansive expression of energy; forming perception, narrative, and self-awareness.

All these layers are simply different frequencies of the same unified field:

THE UNIFIED ENERGY FIELD.

The Axis System was designed to offer a practical yet profound approach to understanding and optimizing the human body's electromagnetic mechanisms, providing tools to regulate, transform, and enhance performance. At its core, this system harmonizes the three primary electromagnetic fields of the human body: the gut, the heart, and the brain. These fields, when synchronized, create a state of coherence that enhances cognition, emotional balance, and physical vitality.

THE THREE ELECTROMAGNETIC FIELDS OF THE HUMAN BODY

Modern research has revealed that the human body generates multiple electromagnetic fields, each playing a role in biological function and self-regulation. The three primary fields (the gut, the heart, and the brain) correspond to the three main divisions of the chakra system: the lower, middle, and upper centers of energy processing.

1. The Gut's Electromagnetic Field (Lower Chakras - Root, Sacral, and Solar Plexus).

Though often overlooked, the gut possesses its own bioelectrical activity, forming what some researchers describe as a "third brain" due to its extensive enteric nervous system (ENS). The ENS is a vast network of over 500 million neurons embedded in the walls of the gastrointestinal tract, influencing digestion, immune function, and emotional processing (Gershon, 1999).

While not as strong as the heart's electromagnetic field, studies suggest that the gut microbiota interacts with electromagnetic waves, affecting bioelectric communication within the body (Funk, 2019). This suggests that the gut field plays a foundational role in grounding the body's energy and ensuring proper metabolic balance.

2. The Heart's Electromagnetic Field (Middle Chakra - Anahata, The Integrator)

The heart generates the most powerful and far-reaching electromagnetic field in the human body, radiating up to 60 times greater in amplitude than the brain's electromagnetic field and extending several feet beyond the body (McCraty et al., 2009). This field is central to emotional regulation, interpersonal connectivity, and physiological coherence.

Studies conducted at the HeartMath Institute have shown that emotional states directly influence the heart's electromagnetic field. Positive emotions such as gratitude and love increase heart coherence, which in turn positively affects cognitive function, stress resilience, and overall well-being (McCraty et al., 2014). This confirms the heart's role as the bridge between the instinctive survival systems of the gut and the cognitive, analytical processes of the brain.

3. The Brain's Electromagnetic Field (Upper Chakras - Throat, Third Eye, and Crown)

The brain's electromagnetic field is produced by neural oscillations, with frequencies ranging from 0.5 Hz to over 100 Hz, governing states of wakefulness, creativity, problem-solving, and deep meditation (Buzsáki, 2006).

The synchronization of neural oscillations between different brain regions (particularly the prefrontal cortex and limbic system) regulates attention, perception, and higher consciousness.

GAMMA WAVES
30-100 Hz

- Higher cognitive functions
- Information processing
- Heightened perception
- Peak concentration and focus

BETA WAVES
12-30 Hz

- Normal waking consciousness
- Active thinking and problem-solving
- Focused mental activity
- Alertness and concentration

ALPHA WAVES
8-12 Hz

- Relaxed alertness
- Calm and peaceful state
- Light meditation
- Daydreaming

THETA WAVES
4-8 Hz

- Light sleep or drowsiness
- Deep meditation
- Creativity and intuition
- Memory formation

DELTA WAVES
0.5 - 4 Hz

- Deep, dreamless sleep
- Healing and regeneration
- Unconsciousness

Neuroscientists have observed that focused attention and meditation can alter the brain's electromagnetic frequencies, increasing coherence between different brainwave states (Lutz et al., 2004). This suggests that conscious regulation of the brain's electromagnetic field can significantly enhance cognitive function and emotional stability.

When these three electromagnetic fields become synchronized, the body enters a state of coherence, leading to enhanced mental clarity, emotional stability, and physiological efficiency. This synchronization can be measured using heart rate variability (HRV), EEG brainwave coherence, and gut microbiota balance (Lacey & Lacey, 1978).

Research has demonstrated that the heart's electromagnetic field can entrain brainwave activity, leading to a state called psychophysiological coherence, where heart rhythms, brainwave patterns, and nervous system functions become synchronized

(Bradley et al., 2008). This coherence increases problem-solving ability, enhances immune response, and optimizes decision-making skills.

Meditation practices that train focused attention have been linked to increased prefrontal cortex activation, greater emotional regulation, and enhanced problem-solving capabilities (Davidson & McEwen, 2012). By cultivating deliberate attention to breath, posture, and energy flow, individuals using the Axis System can consciously regulate their bio-electromagnetic states.

Dr. Bruce Lipton describes the body as a biological tuning system, constantly responding to external and internal electromagnetic influences. He states that conscious regulation of bioelectrical signals can alter gene expression, cellular behavior, and overall health outcomes (Lipton, 2005).

Additional research has confirmed that practices that enhance heart-brain coherence led to greater neuroplasticity, improved immune function, and heightened cognitive performance (McCraty et al., 2009).

These scientific findings validate the ancient wisdom of yoga, breath mastery, and meditative focus, confirming that when practiced systematically, the human body and mind can be trained to operate at peak efficiency: achieving heightened states of awareness, resilience, and performance.

Your energy field determines everything:

• Your vitality, your ability to act, your behavior patterns.

• Your creative force, your ability to manifest.

• Your capacity to evolve, to transcend challenges, and to become the highest version of yourself.

The POWER of your energy field is what determines your ability to create, transform, and transcend.

ENERGY AS THE CURRENCY OF LIFE

Your state of vibration dictates the efficiency of your actions, your clarity of thought, and your ability to navigate life's challenges.

When your energy field is weak, you experience:

• Ambiguity and indecision.

• Creative blocks and stagnation.

• Easily being influenced by external forces.

When your energy field is strong, you experience:

• Clear direction and deep focus.

• A seamless connection between your thoughts, emotions, and actions.

• An expanded ability to shape your reality.

To put it simply:

Your capacity to solve problems, respond to life, and evolve beyond limitations is conditioned by the strength of your vital force. This is why posture, breath, and attention matter so much, because they are the factors that determine our state of vibration, and our experience by consequence. Remember that you will only experience that which you are resonant with; your vibration determines the outcome of your experience.

The Axis system is about how to generate, sustain, direct and amplify energy to fulfill your purpose.

But… what purpose?

What is the purpose of human life?

Everything in this book has led to this one question…

Why do we cultivate energy?

What do we want to be healthy for? What's the point of all this effort?

And the answer is simple yet infinite:

The purpose of human experience is to unveil the nature and potential of your existence to its highest degree of possibility.

That is why you are here.

Your role is not to simply exist; it is to unveil yourself, to unfold into your highest possible state.

This is the essence of self-realization, the very foundation of mysticism, yoga, and all conscious paths of awakening.

As Rumi once said:

"You are not a drop of water in the ocean. You are the entire ocean within a drop."

I like to say it like this:

"We are nature, God's imagination creating and experiencing itself."

And so, the greatest work you can do is to awaken to the truth of who you are and to bring that truth into expression with full force.

THE REALITY OF POWER & INFLUENCE

We live in a world that operates on power and influence, this is an undeniable. Indeed, this is a law of nature, the same law that structures the hierarchy of the bee hives, the wolf packs, the rainforest canopies, the solar systems and the star clusters. Everything is fields within fields, energy vibrating at a certain frequency and organizing the particles of space in order of magnitude and resonance. This structure of hierarchy is a manifestation of nature's intelligence, and we must learn to play within its laws and equations.

History has shown us that:

• Power is not about being good or bad; it is about force and presence.

• The world doesn't operate based on the written rules, but based on the laws nature, based on powers and principalities.

• The world does not reward passive potential, it rewards those who cultivate and direct their energy into conscious persistent action.

This is why many who lack good intentions have gained massive success and why many with pure intentions have suffered failure. This happens all the time and it's because nature does not judge morality, it responds to energy, movement, and power.

This is not an argument for abandoning ethics or principles, it is the opposite. It is an understanding that if you want to be an agent of positive transformation, you must develop enough energy, strength, and focus to withstand the world's forces and influence reality with your vision.

To do this, you must:

• Refine your posture so that your body is aligned and primed for action.

• Master your breath so that your energy remains steady, balanced, and powerful.

• Control your attention so that you do not become distracted, manipulated, or lost in the chaos of external narratives.

SELF-RESPONSIBILITY: THE FOUNDATION OF MASTERY

If there is one core truth that all mysticism shares, it is this:

You are responsible for everything.

Everything you experience is a result of the choices you have made, the perspectives you have held, and the energy you have cultivated.

This is not a burden; **it is the ultimate freedom.**

When you take full responsibility for your state of being, you unlock the ability to reshape your reality at will.

You realize that:

• Every challenge in your life is consequence of a decision you made, and it's there to awaken you to a higher potential experience.

• Every difficulty is an opportunity to extract strength, power and wisdom from the pressures in the process of transformation.

• Every moment is an invitation to claim your power or surrender it to external forces.

The question is not:

"What does life want from me?"

The question is:

"What do I want from life?"

This is because experience is generated from within!

THE KEY TO YOUR TRUE SIGNATURE VIBRATION:

AUTHENTICITY

Your core signature vibration is the most unique and unrepeatable aspect of your existence.

"There has never been, and there will never be, another you."

Not one single being in the infinite history of the universe has had your exact:

• Perception.

• Emotional depth.

• Creative expression.

• Unique blend of strengths and wisdom.

You are indispensable, not because the world needs you, but because you are a once-in-eternity moment that can never be replicated.

The most important thing for a mystic to understand is this:

You are a singular expression of consciousness. Your perspective, your voice, your experience, this will never exist again. And so, the highest duty you have is to fully embody the gift of your own existence.

This is why self-realization is not just philosophy; **it is urgency**.

Because **Memento Mori** (the reminder of death) is the most powerful teacher.

If life is fleeting, then let's live in the most powerful way possible.

So that when the time comes, we have no regrets of having lived lesser than what was possible.

PART III

THE AXIS FUTURE

CHAPTER X

THE CHAKRAS

चक्र

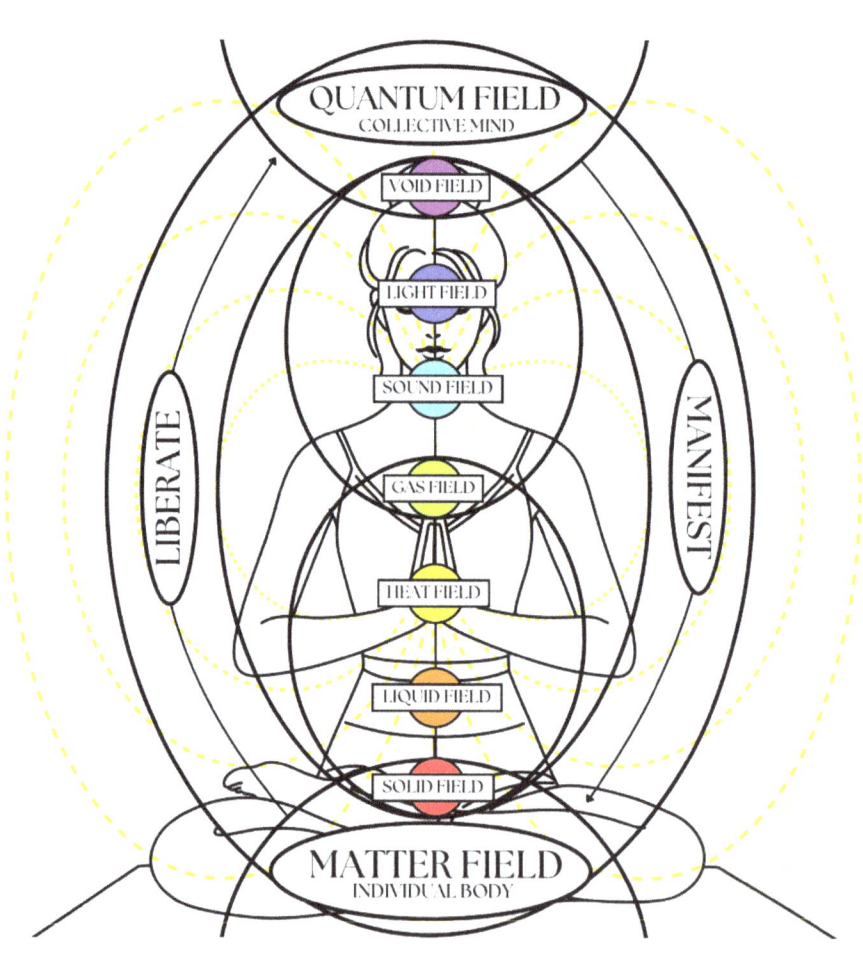

THE VORTEXES OF ENERGY PROCESSING

The word Chakra (चक्र) means "wheel" or "vortex" in Sanskrit. A chakra is a spinning field of energy where opposing forces: Gravity (Ida - Shakti) and Willpower (Pingala - Shiva) meet and spiral to create the force of life, which expresses as the electromagnetic toroidal fields of consciousness.

- Ida (इडा) - The feminine, gravitational, receptive energy associated with introspection and emotions, the negative charge of the field.
- Pingala (पिङ्गल) - The masculine, radiant, heating energy associated with action, expression, and willpower, the positive charge.

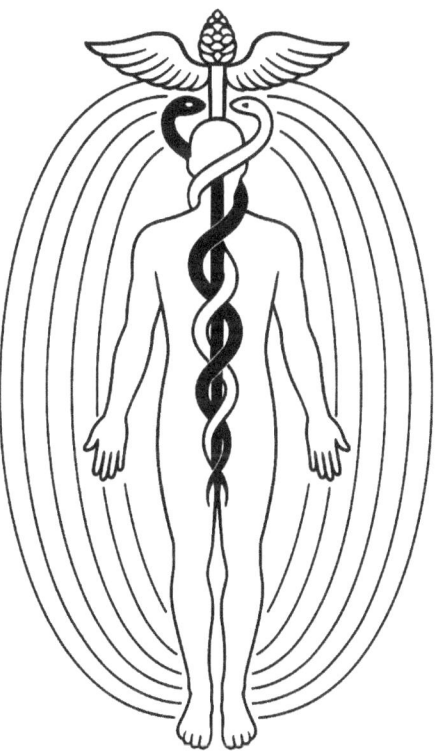

These two energetic currents spiral around each other, forming a double-helix pattern, weaving through the Sushumna Nadi (सुषुम्ना नाड़ी): the central axis that connects all chakras along the spine.

Each chakra is a vortex where these forces intersect, acting as an energetic processing center for perception, experience, and emotion. Making the chakra system the core of the processing of experience, the axis of the Self where physical, emotional, and mental fields converge to create the human experience.

117

The chakras govern how we feel, how we process life, and how we express our energy. So, if you want to become healthier, powerful and happy, you must understand the nature of this ancient system and how to use it to ascend your life experience. Let's begin and explore each chakra in depth.

THE SEVEN CHAKRAS:

मूलाधार

Muladhara
(Root Chakra)

The Solid Spectrum of Energy.

"A tree cannot grow tall without strong roots"

Your sense of security is the foundation for all higher expression.

Sanskrit Name: मूलाधार (Mūlādhāra)

Name Meaning: *Mula* (root) + *Adhara* (support/base) = "Root Support".

Element: Earth (पृथ्वी / Pṛthvī)

Vibrational State (AXIS): Solid spectrum of energy

Emotion: Fear ↔ Confidence

Location: Base of spine (coccyx/perineum)

Color: Red

Sound/Mantra: "Lam"

Musical Note: C

Nerve Plexus: Inferior hypogastric plexus

Primary Function: Survival, grounding, structure

Body Systems: Legs, feet, skeletal structure, sphincters, elimination

THE FOUNDATION OF EMBODIED ENERGY

The Muladhara chakra, or root chakra, represents the base of the human energetic structure. It is where consciousness crystallizes into matter, forming the foundation of the body's physical and psychological stability. In classical systems, it is linked to the earth element; in the AXIS system, it is reinterpreted as the solid spectrum of energy; a symbolic and scientific reference to the densest vibrational field in the human system. This spectrum includes the gravitational pull that binds the body to the earth, the rigidity of skeletal form, and the slow-moving resonance of survival instinct.

Anatomically, Muladhara is rooted in the pelvic floor and the base of the spine, connected to the legs and feet (the body's primary points of contact with the earth). The "Ida" and "Pingala" nadis, subtle energetic channels that carry lunar and solar energies, rise from the soles of the feet and spiral upward along the legs. At the coccyx, they intersect and create the energetic fusion that forms the Muladhara chakra. From here, the central channel: "Sushumna" emerges, becoming the axis along which all the other chakras align. In this way, Muladhara is not just the first chakra; it is the anchor point for the entire vertical structure of the self.

THE PSYCHOLOGY OF GROUNDING AND SURVIVAL

The Muladhara chakra governs our core survival programs: the instinct to fight, flee, freeze, or adapt in the face of danger. It houses the unconscious blueprint we inherit around safety, tribe, home, and belonging.

When this chakra is balanced, we feel grounded, connected to our environment, and capable of moving through life with security and strength. When it is imbalanced, fear and anxiety arise (often expressed as hypervigilance, disconnection from the body, or a compulsive attachment to material security).

On the physiological level, this chakra corresponds with the inferior hypogastric plexus, a complex nerve network governing elimination and reproductive functions. It is also linked to electromagnetic patterns at the base of the spine.

Practices like deep pelvic breathing, standing postures, and low-frequency vibration (chanting "Lam") help to stimulate and stabilize this energetic base. Grounding rituals, mindful walking, and movement practices that engage the lower body strengthen the root, supporting a stable foundation for higher energy centers to awaken.

The Muladhara chakra is where the journey begins. Before we can expand, evolve, or ascend, we must anchor. Rootedness is not rigidity; it is the readiness to rise with power, precision, and presence.

MULADHARA ACTIVATION PRACTICE:

ROOTING INTO THE GROUND

To harmonize and activate the first chakra, you must return to the foundation of your existence: *support*. The primary need of the system is not food, nor even air, it is structural integrity. Without support, nothing can rise. And in the human system, **true support begins at the perineum**.

The Exercise: Root Axis Awareness

1. **Center Your Attention**: Bring your awareness to the **perineum** (the central point at the base of the pelvis). This is the seat of Muladhara, the gate of embodiment.

2. **Feel the Connection to Earth**: From the perineum, extend your consciousness **downward through your legs**, tracing the energetic pathways (meridians) into the soles of your feet. Imagine the **earth rising to meet you** as you stand.

3. **Balance the Four Directions of Support**: Begin to refine your perception of how weight distributes from your perineum:
   o Right and left leg
   o Front of the foot (ball and toes) and back of the foot (heel)

Let the **weight settle evenly**, creating a sense of equilibrium. If you feel more weight on one side, gently adjust by transferring the weight from one hemisphere to the other; not with force, but with presence.

4. **Align the Axis**: As you distribute the weight, allow your spine to **respond naturally**. You are not holding yourself up; **you are allowing the earth to support you**. This is rooting. This is trust.

5. **Breathe Into the Root**: Breathe deeply into the base of the pelvis. As your breath slows and deepens, your **nervous system settles**, your **wavelength elongates**, and your **state of consciousness expands**. The lower and calmer your breath, the broader the **wave span of awareness** you can hold.

You will begin to feel that the more evenly you distribute your weight, the more support you create; the more stable your structure, the more **gracefully you hold yourself**, and the more **powerfully and confidently you radiate** your presence.

As a result, your environment will **perceive you differently**. Rooted and regulated, you emanate **a field of steadiness and trust**. You become someone others recognize, *not just as grounded, but as gravitational.*

स्वाधिष्ठान

Swadhisthana
(Sacral Chakra)

The Liquid Spectrum of Energy

"To flow with life is to dance with its waters"

Rigidity drowns, but adaptability thrives.

Sanskrit Name: स्वाधिष्ठान (Svādhiṣṭhāna)

Name Meaning: *Sva* (self)+*Adhisthana* (dwelling place)= One's Own Abode

Element: Water (**अप** / Apas)

Vibrational State (AXIS): Liquid spectrum of energy

Emotion: Suffering ↔ Pleasure

Location: Lower abdomen, sacrum, reproductive organs

Color: Orange

Sound/Mantra: "Vam"

Musical Note: D

Nerve Plexus: Sacral plexus

Primary Function: Emotion, pleasure, creativity, relationship

Body Systems: Reproductive organs, kidneys, bladder, lymphatic and circulatory fluids

THE WATERS OF LIFE AND MOTION

Svadhisthana, the second chakra in the energetic system, is the seat of fluidity; both literal and symbolic. Its name, from the Sanskrit *Sva* (self) and *Adhisthana* (dwelling place), evokes the image of a sacred space where the individual self begins to interact with the world through sensation, desire, and movement. If the root chakra grounds us in existence, Svadhisthana is the first ripple of that existence expressing itself. In classical systems, it is aligned with the water element: sensations, flow, adaptability, life. In the AXIS system, this chakra corresponds to the liquid spectrum of energy, representing the dynamic, circulating flow that moves within and around us.

Located just below the navel, this chakra governs the lower abdomen, pelvic basin, and organs responsible for reproduction, and hormonal communication. Physiologically, it corresponds to the sacral plexus, a nerve network that integrates sensory, motor, and autonomic signals within the pelvic region. Energetically, Svadhisthana is the field of emotional memory and sensuality. It holds the imprint of past relationships and inherited emotional patterns, shaping our intimacy, creativity, and capacity to feel deeply. It is in this watery domain that our boundaries are first tested, and where we begin to open to others through connection, rhythm, and desire.

CREATIVITY, PLEASURE, AND EMOTIONAL FLOW

The energy of Svadhisthana is not simply sexual; it is the charge of creation itself, the urge to give form to feeling and to shape beauty from impulse. It is the space where movement becomes dance, longing becomes poetry, and breath becomes expression. A balanced second chakra brings ease in emotional expression, comfort in the body, and a fluid responsiveness to life's changes. An imbalance here may manifest as emotional rigidity, sexual repression, dependency, or overindulgence.

Its vibrational key is the Bija mantra "Vam." Vocalizing this sound, especially during practices like seated pelvic meditation or hip-opening yoga postures, helps activate its frequencies. Scientific correlations (though still speculative) suggest the chakra's location corresponds to hormonal and lymphatic regulation. Moreover, fluid-based systems like blood, lymph, and cerebrospinal fluid reflect the second chakra's symbolic role as an energetic circulatory force.

To nourish Svadhisthana, engage in creative acts without the need for perfection. Dance, sing, paint, or simply feel. Practice yoga postures such as Baddha Konasana (Bound Angle Pose) or Utkata Konasana (Goddess Pose) to stimulate the hips and pelvic basin. Hydrate well, swim, move your hips, and let your emotions be acknowledged rather than judged.

Svadhisthana reminds us that the self is not a fixed form, but a wave capable of joy, sensitivity, and change. When we honor its movement, we begin to trust the flow of life within us.

SVADHISTHANA ACTIVATION PRACTICE:

THE ALCHEMY OF SENSATION

To activate the second chakra, we must enter the realm of **fluid sensation**, the place where emotion, digestion, and perception blend. Svadhisthana is the seat of emotional memory and metabolic intelligence. It governs how we **process sensations, the liquid aspect of experience**, particularly through the **gut and sexual organs**.

The Exercise: Emotional Digestion Through Presence

1. **Place Your Hands**: Bring your hands together and gently **cup the sacral area** resting the palms on the soft space between your navel and genitals. This is the gateway to your internal waters, where digestion and emotional alchemy occur.

2. **Calm the Breath**: Begin to breathe; not slowly, but **calmly**. Let your breath move with its natural rhythm, yet make it **silent**. No force, no sound. Only the **kindness of breath** flowing in and out of your system.

3. **Dive Into the Inner Waters**: As you hold this space, allow your **attention to sink beneath the skin**, into the subtle landscape of your intestines, bladder, and reproductive organs. These organs are not just biological, they are **emotional reservoirs**, holding stories and sensations in flux.

4. **Feel Without Interpretation**: As you tune in, you will likely feel discomfort, tightness, or turbulence. Do **not interpret**

these sensations. Do not say *"I feel bad."* Instead, recognize: *"There is a sensation arising in my gut."* This distinction is essential.

When we confuse sensation with self, we become **entangled**. But when we witness sensation as sensation, we create **space for transmutation**.

5. **Acknowledge and Allow**: The purpose of this practice is **not to fix, react, or escape**. It is simply to **acknowledge**, to sit in presence with your internal experience. Just as your body digests food, your system also digests emotion. The way you metabolize feeling mirrors the way you process matter.

6. **Transmute Through Awareness**: By staying present with these sensations (without turning away, without judgment) you begin to **irrigate the inner field with attention**. And attention is a catalyst.

Your feelings are not problems. They are **processes**; liquid movements of intelligence passing through your body. When you stop trying to *feel better* and simply *feel deeper*, you unlock your natural capacity to **digest experience** and restore inner harmony.

मणिपूर

Manipura
(Solar Plexus)

The Fire of Will and Vibrational Integration

"Awake the vital energy from within"

Sanskrit Name: मणिपूर (Maṇipūra)

Name Meaning: *Mani* (jewel) + *Pura* (city) = "City of Jewels"

Element: Fire (**तेजस्** / Tejas)

Vibrational State (AXIS): Heat / Thermodynamic force

Emotion: Stagnation ↔ Power

Location: Solar plexus (just above the navel), stomach.

Color: Yellow

Sound/Mantra: "Ram"

Musical Note: E

Nerve Plexus: Celiac (solar) plexus

Primary Function: Will, transformation, perception

Body Systems: Digestive system, liver, pancreas, adrenals.

THE ENGINE OF SELF-TRANSFORMATION

Manipura, the third chakra, is the fiery center of power, digestion, and identity. Situated in the solar plexus (the great sun of the human body, three fingers above the navel) this chakra is traditionally associated with fire and transformation. In the AXIS system, Manipura is understood as more than just the element of fire; it is the **thermodynamic force** that governs the vibration of consciousness itself. It is not merely one part of consciousness; it is the integration of all its parts.

As such, Manipura is the vibrational frequency through which consciousness determines its state of expression; whether it manifests in a solid, liquid, gas, sound, light, or void-like frequency; it's all the same, motion, energy, vibration: Consciousness.

This is why Manipura is so intimately linked to human willpower. Will is not simply intention, it is the internal temperature that shapes the movement of thought into form. It is the flame that quickens perception, decision-making, metabolism, and transformation.

The very way we feel ourselves to be (the self-image we hold as inner identity) radiates from this chakra. And just as heat can turn ice to water and water to vapor, the will within Manipura can transmute our consciousness from one state to another. Through will, we do not just change how we act; we change how we *are*, and in doing so, we unlock new modes of perception and possibility.

DIGESTION, DIRECTION, AND THE POWER TO CHOOSE

On the physiological level, Manipura governs the digestive system: the stomach, pancreas, liver, and intestines. It is linked to the **celiac plexus**, often called the solar plexus, a dense web of nerves that regulates stress responses, gut intelligence, and metabolic fire. This center not only digests food but also life experience. It is here that we transform what we take in (nutrients, emotions and ideas) into usable energy.

This makes Manipura the home of our inner alchemist: the one who extracts meaning, strength, and purpose from the raw material of life.

The color yellow radiates from this chakra like sunlight, signaling vitality, discernment, and brightness of spirit. The musical note E and the Bija mantra "Ram" resonate with Manipura's frequency. Breathing into the diaphragm, allowing the belly to expand and contract with rhythm and control, also supports the healthy function of this center.

Emotionally, Manipura governs self-esteem, assertiveness, and clarity of purpose. A balanced solar plexus chakra allows us to take initiative, set boundaries, and act with conviction. When imbalanced, it may manifest as insecurity, shame, aggression, or paralysis. But at its highest expression, Manipura gives rise to sovereignty: the power to center oneself in truth, in order to shape one's reality through focused intention into action, to rise above conditioned identity into deliberate being.

This chakra holds the secret of transformation because it is the measure and modulator of vibration. It is the calibrator of experience. When will is clear, the entire system aligns. When heat is balanced, life flows with purpose. In the solar fire of Manipura, the jewel of choice is revealed: we become the authors of who we are becoming.

MANIPURA ACTIVATION PRACTICE:

IGNITING THE WILL THROUGH THE AXIS OF MOTION

At the core of the third chakra's fire is the **diaphragm**: the physical and energetic gateway between the upper and lower torso.

The diaphragm separates the lungs and heart (our emotional and respiratory rhythms) from the organs of digestion, which are responsible for converting matter into usable energy.

The Exercise: Rhythmic Jumping to Center the Fire

1. **Stand in Your Axis**: Begin in a grounded, upright position. Align your posture according to the principles of the AXIS system: feet evenly rooted, knees soft, spine extended, and head floating lightly above the body.

2. **Initiate the Bounce**: Start by gently bending the knees, allowing your body's weight to rise and fall in a light bounce. Keep the soles of your feet grounded at first. Feel the wave of motion traveling through your spine.

3. **Release the Heels**: When you feel steady, begin to lift your heels, letting the body gently leave the ground. These are micro-jumps; small, soft, rhythmic pulses designed to stimulate the core without strain.

4. **Build the Rhythm**: As your confidence and coordination grow, increase the height of the jumps slightly, and allow them to become rhythmic. Synchronize the movement with your breath:

- o **Inhale on the descent**
- o **Exhale on the lift**

This creates a circuit of fire and air, fueling the system with breath as you build kinetic momentum.

5. **Center the Diaphragm**: Bring your attention to the diaphragm, about two to three fingers above the navel. As you continue jumping, gently draw this area inward and upward toward the spine, anchoring your movement in the core of your being.

6. **Freeze and Harness the Energy**: After a full round of activation, suddenly stop. Stand completely still, freeze the motion. You may feel a rush of internal energy, vibrations, or even turbulence. This is your system recalibrating. Breathe calmly. Hold your Axis. Allow your structure to integrate the activation.

7. **Return to Stillness, Return to Power**: As your breath returns to its natural rhythm, notice the change:
   - o Your focus is sharper.
   - o Your center is stronger.
   - o Your resolve is clearer.

Now that your Manipura Chakra, The Heat Field, is activated you have the opportunity to freely direct your energy to whichever endeavor is relevant to your consciousness and path. Remember that this activation must be always followed by **Determined Action**, otherwise it may lead to increased stress and anxiety. The activation of the Heat Field may feel uncomfortable as one becomes used to its own power and energy. Enjoy the process and train regularly to see bigger results.

अनाहत.

Anahata
(Heart Chakra)

The Center of the Human Experience

"The heart is the vortex where heaven meets earth"

This is the nucleus of human experience, the place where mind meets flesh.

Sanskrit Name: अनाहत (Anāhata)

Name Meaning: *Anahata* – "Unstruck" or "Unbeaten"= "Unstruck Sound"

Element: Air (**वायु** / Vāyu)

Vibrational State (AXIS): Gas / Atmosphere

Emotion: Hate ↔ Love.

Location: Center of the chest, heart, lungs, thymus gland

Color: Green

Sound/Mantra: "Yam"

Musical Note: F

Nerve Plexus: Cardiac plexus

Primary Function: Psychosomatic integration, love, balance

Body Systems: Heart, lungs, circulatory system, thymus gland, lymphatic network.

THE BRIDGE BETWEEN SKY AND EARTH

Anahata, the fourth chakra, is the nexus of the human energy system, the point where the subtle and tangible meet. Just as the Earth itself is composed of a solid core, liquid mantle, and gaseous atmosphere, the body holds within it a mirror of this layered reality.

The root, sacral, and solar plexus chakras are like the Earth, and express the tangible aspects of consciousness: physicality, sensation, digestion, and vital force.

The throat, brow, and crown chakras are like the firmament (the outer space), and they reflect the subtle, abstract realms of perception, language, vision, and pure awareness.

Anahata is the in-between, the Gas Field that mediates as the atmosphere between Earth and Outer Space, is the moment of intersection where spirit becomes breath, and body senses becomes concept and meaning.

In ancient Greek terms, the three upper chakras correspond to the *psyche* (mind), and the three lower chakras to the *soma* (body). The Anahata chakra is where these two meet, defining the essence of human experience: the psychosomatic union. It is not merely a center of love or compassion in the emotional sense; it is the anatomical and energetic meeting point that makes the human experience possible.

Centered at the sternum, it corresponds to the thymus gland, which governs the immune system and lies at the heart of the lymphatic system (the fluidic web responsible for cleansing emotional and hormonal waste, regulating vitality, and harmonizing the inner terrain). Through this lens, the heart is not only the emotional core, but the alchemical center where creation and acceptance merge.

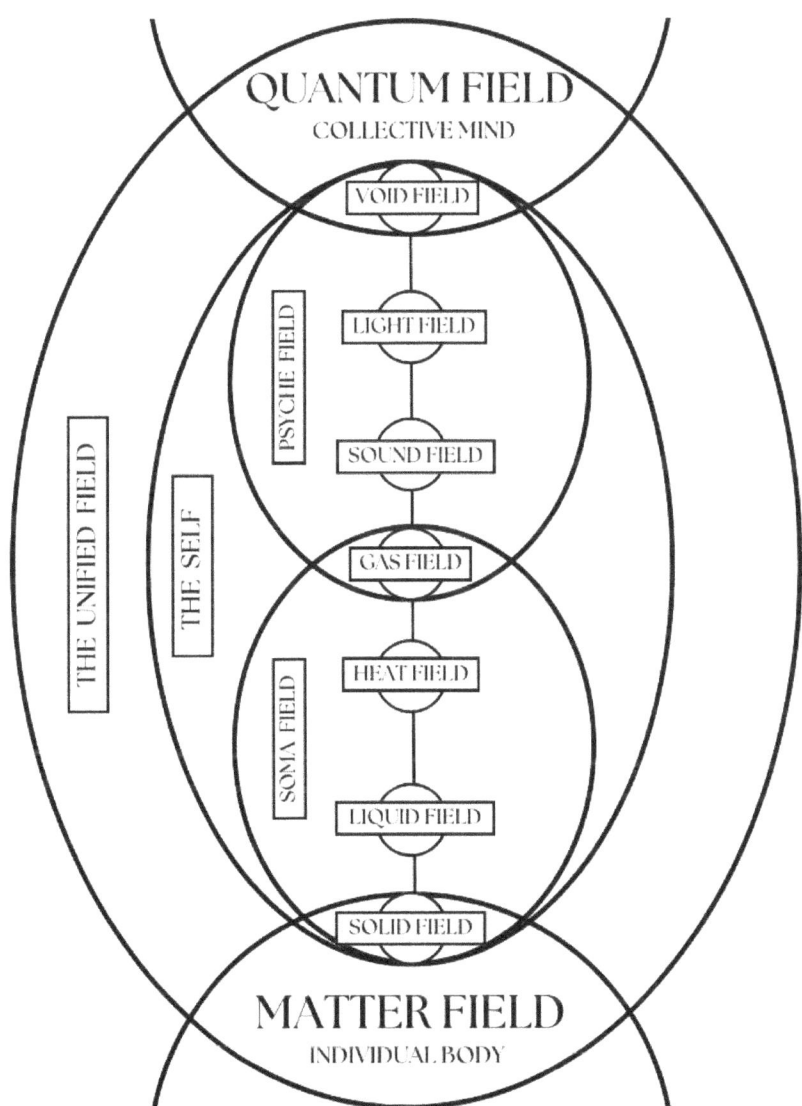

THE GEOMETRY OF INTEGRATION

Symbolically, Anahata is represented by two interlocking triangles (one pointing upward, the other downward) forming a six-pointed star or hexagram.

This image reflects the balance between gravity and willpower, between the descending pull of nature and the ascending drive of intention. It also appears in the Star of David, the Metatron's Cube, and in the Seed and Flower of Life, structures that underpin natural architecture from beehives to molecular bonds.

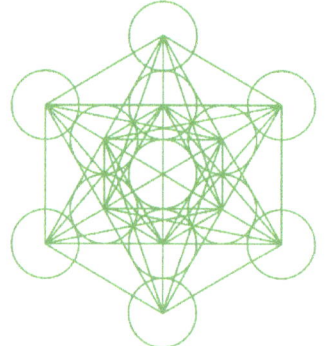

METATRON'S CUBE

The number four, which defines this chakra's position, is not arbitrary: four is the number of form and structure, it is seen in the four chambers of the heart, the four directions, and the four limbs that extend from this center. The heart, through its ventricles, arms, and ribs, expands into the world as the architecture of giving and receiving.

Human beings are the only mammals who consistently walk upright, turning the spine into a living antenna, a connection that allows Humans to experience the spectrum between the Quantum and Matter Fields of consciousness.

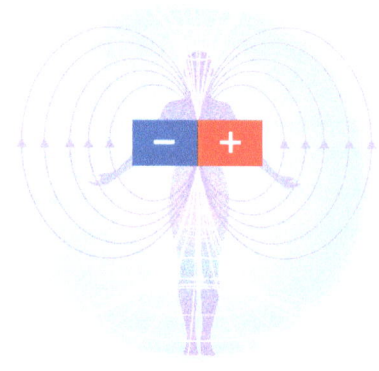

This verticality grants us not just bipedal mobility, but access to the simultaneous reception of gravity and transmission of will through our hands and arms (extensions of these Chakra). In Anahata, these forces meet and harmonize. Our posture, our breath, our emotional resonance, all are mediated by the thymic space at the chest. And through our arms and hands, we touch, create, offer, and hold. These actions are not simply physical, they are sacred technologies of psychosomatic connection.

Anahata is where we process not only how we are loved, but how we choose to love. It is where we metabolize emotional experience and learn to respond rather than react. It is the seat of empathy, but also the gate of energetic discernment. Here, in the green resonance of air and openness, we realize that life is both something we receive and something we shape.

ANAHATA ACTIVATION PRACTICE:

TOUCHING THE WORLD WITH KINDNESS

The first three chakras are about the self (your survival, your sensation, your will). But **Anahata**, the fourth chakra, marks a shift. It is the **bridge between self and All**, between your personal singular experience and the quantum web of life that surrounds and supports your individual existence.

Anahata is about relationship. It governs your ability to love, to give, to receive, and to live in harmony with the world. And the most immediate, most powerful way you relate to the world every day is through your **hands**.

The Exercise: Conscious Touch as Relational Activation

1. **Acknowledge the Role of Your Hands**: Your hands are **extensions of your heart**.
   - o   You greet people with a handshake.
   - o   You comfort with a caress.
   - o   You create with a brush, a pen, an instrument.
   - o   You express affection, make offerings, and shape reality with your touch.

Most of what you do in the world is done **through your hands**.

2. **Activate Through Action**: To harmonize the fourth chakra, **do something with your hands**, but do it consciously.
   - o   Pet your animal.
   - o   Draw, paint, write.
   - o   Massage a loved one.
   - o   Hug someone and mean it.
   - o   Play the drums or any instrument.
   - o   Plant something.
   - o   Wash dishes.

- o Give, serve, create.

Whatever you do, make sure you **bring kindness to the act of motion**.

3. **Refine Your Touch**: Observe how you touch.
   - o Is it rushed or present?
   - o Is it cold or warm?
   - o Is it mechanical or infused with care?

You don't have to be gentle all the time; life has its intensities. But kindness should be the **core frequency** that guides your contact with others.

4. **Balance, Don't Burn**: Like all chakras, Anahata is a potential, not a moral label.
   - o Too little activation, and love becomes cold, withheld, or numb.
   - o Too much activation, and you burn out when overextending, overgiving, losing center.

Harmony in the heart comes from sustainable motion, not stillness, not excess, but from flow. Engage enough to stay warm, release enough to stay light.

Anahata reminds us: the way you touch the world reflects the way you love it. And the way you love the world reflects the way you know yourself.

So, use your hands not just to act, but to *relate*. And let every gesture be an offering of presence.

विशुद्ध

Vishuddha
(Throat Chakra)

"The sound of your Vibrational signature"

The Voice of Truth and Singularity

Sanskrit Name: विशुद्ध (Viśuddha)

Name Meaning: *Vishuddha* – "Purification" or "Pure" = "Pure Expression"

Element: Ether / Space (आकाश / Ākāśa)

Vibrational State (AXIS): Gravity / Vibrational resonance

Emotion: Illusion ↔ Truth

Location: Throat, vocal cords, larynx, thyroid gland.

Color: Aquamarine

Sound/Mantra: "Ham"

Musical Note: G

Nerve Plexus: Cervical plexus

Primary Function: Expression, authenticity, vibration

Body Systems: Respiratory tract, vocal cords, thyroid/parathyroid glands

THE VALVE OF AUTHENTIC EXPRESSION

Vishuddha, the fifth chakra, sits at the base of the throat, functioning as both a passage and a portal. In many ways, it is the most paradoxical of all energy centers: singular in structure, yet capable of infinite resonance. While the human body is largely built in pairs (two eyes, ears, lungs, kidneys, hemispheres of the brain) the throat stands as one. A singular channel. A narrow, central valve. And through this opening, the uniqueness of our being is voiced into the world.

If the first four chakras help us root, connect, and belong, Vishuddha represents the threshold of individuation. It is where our singularity becomes audible. It is where we begin to understand that our voice is not just sound, it is a vibration shaped by our muscles, our choices, and our history. The texture of someone's voice, their inflections, pauses, rhythm, and breath, all reveal the emotional story of their body and the alignment of their truth. To speak authentically is to reveal the frequency of one's soul.

RESPONSIBILITY, RESONANCE, AND THE POWER OF VOICE

To live in truth is not a passive state, it is an active and conscious practice. The voice must be cultivated like a muscle and tuned like an instrument. In many traditions, chanting is not merely spiritual, it is a corrective, clinical and social way of bonding, creating and healing. The sound "Ham," when vocalized with awareness, clears the subtle passage of the throat and strengthens the connection between the head and the heart. Breathwork, toning, singing, and speech refinement are all tools that awaken Vishuddha.

The nerve structure surrounding the throat, particularly the cervical plexus and Vagus nerve, play a key role in autonomic function and communication between brain and body. The thyroid and parathyroid glands govern metabolism and calcium regulation; both deeply tied to self-regulation and vitality.

A balanced fifth chakra brings clear communication, integrity, and creative fluency. When underactive, it may express as silence, insecurity, or fear of judgment. When overactive, it may manifest as dogmatism, manipulation, or speech divorced from heart and wisdom.

Vishuddha is not just a center for expression and voice, it should be understood as a *responsibility* to embody our uniqueness with precision and care into the world. Through it, we articulate the formless into the formed. We give shape to the unseen. The throat is the conduit through which the psyche becomes action and idea becomes relationship, and in this way, it is the gatekeeper of manifestation.

At its essence, Vishuddha is not only a center of communication but of purification. In order to speak true words, the energy that moves through us must be clear. In order to receive insight from above and transmit it below, we must remain open. The fifth chakra is not simply about sound; it is a vow to yourself and the world as a creator. A vow to carry the true authentic presence of who you are into the world, through breath, speech, sound, and resonance.

VISHUDDHA ACTIVATION PRACTICE:

SPEAKING THE TRUTH INTO EXISTENCE

In the AXIS system, we activate this chakra not merely by chanting mantras or humming vibrations, but by **speaking your actual truth out loud**!

Your voice is your code. The more honest and intentional your voice, the more precise your personal vibration becomes. That is how you program reality.

The Exercise: The Voice of the Prayer

To activate Vishuddha, sit in stillness and answer the following three questions in this exact order. Write them with presence. Then speak them aloud. This is your prayer:

1. **What am I grateful for?** Gratitude aligns you with receptivity. It opens the channel and tunes your signal to the frequency of abundance.

2. **What can I do to make life better for myself and the world?**
    This is your service, the recognition that your existence holds value because of what you offer. It places you in alignment with the universal mind, the collective intelligence that only keeps what is useful.

3. **What do I want from experience?** This is your reward, what you seek to receive as a result of your gratitude and service. It is your honest desire, your longing made sacred through clarity.

Once written, read these words aloud. But don't just read; speak with an intentional tone. Let your voice carry feeling. You can sing it, chant it, or recite it like an invocation. What matters is that you emotionally relate to what you are saying.

Because in Vishuddha, it is not just the word that holds power, it is the tone.

- The word is the meaning.
- The tone is the power. Together, they are the alchemy of creation.

This is what the Kabbalists encoded in the sacred phrase: **"Avrah KaDabra"** = **"I will create as I speak."** Derived from ancient Aramaic, *Avrah* means "I will create," and *KaDabra* means "as I speak." It is not superstition, it is the science of vibration, the original magic of intentional speech. By speaking your truth aloud, you are activating the formula of creation itself.

You are not just saying what you want, you are becoming what you speak. And when you speak your truth with clarity and resonance, you declare yourself to the world and to your own nervous system.

This is not metaphorical. This is vibrational programming. You are not born with meaning. You are born to give meaning to life. This is the singularity of sovereignty: to declare your truth, in voice and in vibration, to shape the field around you.

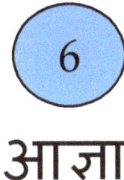

आज्ञा

Ajna
(Third Eye)

The Eye of Intention and the Desire to Experience.

Sanskrit Name: आज्ञा (Ājñā)

Name Meaning: *Ajna* – "Command" or "Perception" = "Command Center"

Element: Light

Vibrational State (AXIS): Time/Light

Emotion: Doubt ↔ Faith

Location: Between the eyebrows, pituitary gland.

Color: Indigo

Sound/Mantra: "Om"

Musical Note: A

Nerve Center: Pituitary gland

Primary Function: Desire, inner vision, mental programming

Body Systems: Brain hemispheres, frontal cortex, endocrine regulation

THE DESIRE THAT CREATES REALITY

Ajna, the sixth chakra, often called the "third eye," is the gateway to inner vision and mental sovereignty. It is located between the eyebrows and is the bridge between the left and right hemispheres of the brain. It is ruled by the **pituitary gland**, the conductor of the endocrine system, and one of the most powerful regulators of the human experience. The pituitary gland wants to experience. That is its nature. It is the biological expression of desire.

This desire is not random, it reflects the core impulse of the universe itself. In Hermetic philosophy, the source of all creation is described as the "mind of the all." And what drives that mind? Desire! The will to create, to know, to become! That same pattern plays out within us.

Ajna is the spark of will within the psyche. If left unconscious, it becomes programmable. What we long for can be shaped by culture, trauma, family, media and trend, so that we spend our lives chasing experiences that serve someone else's business agenda. That is why Ajna is sacred. To use it well is to reclaim the authorship of your reality.

The pituitary's desire activates the **frontal cortex**, the brain's visionary engine, this is where ideas are born. These ideas are crafted from memory and imagination.

Memory offers the raw material: impressions, lessons, images from the past. Imagination reorganizes those fragments into something new. The two are inseparable. Every act of remembering requires imagining, and every act of imagining draws from our memory. In Ajna, memory and imagination become one fluid loop, cycling through the lens of desire to generate the story we believe in.

THE BLUEPRINT OF MANIFESTATION

Ajna is where reality begins. Here, a vision forms, once that vision crystallizes, the chakra system engages.

The sixth chakra projects a mental image. The fifth, Vishuddha, gives it voice. The fourth, Anahata, shapes it into emotion and connection. The third, Manipura, fuels it with willpower and action. The second, Svadhisthana, anchors it into sensation. And the first, Muladhara, solidifies it into tangible experience. This is the true movement of consciousness from subtle to solid, from thought to action.

Understanding Ajna means recognizing that your experience of life is not simply happening to you. It is unfolding through you. What you desire, you imagine. What you imagine, you pursue. What you pursue, you create. But if you do not become conscious of your inner programming, that whole chain of manifestation can serve illusions rather than your truth. The world you live in begins in the architecture of your mind.

The sixth chakra also governs **time**. It lives between memory and projection. To reside in Ajna is to stand in the command center of the psyche, with the power to reflect on the past and reach into the future, while remaining rooted in the present moment, where new choices always become possible.

When Ajna is in balance, clarity reigns. Imagination becomes a tool of alignment. Decision-making becomes precise. You trust your vision. But when this center is blocked or distorted, confusion arises. You may become overwhelmed with ideas but unable to act; or, worse, caught in mental loops that were never truly your own.

To awaken Ajna is to restore sovereignty over the lens through which you see. It is the chakra of orientation, of inner command. It is not only your eye, it is your compass. From it, you shape not just what you want, but who you are.

AJNA ACTIVATION PRACTICE:

PLACING THE WITNESS IN THE CENTER

Ajna, the sixth chakra, is not just about seeing, it is about knowing. It governs the placement of attention, the convergence of memory and imagination, and the conscious authorship of your internal narrative.

There are infinite ways to activate Ajna, but they all begin in the same place: **stillness**.

The Exercise: Deep Presence and Conscious Visioning

1. **Sit Down. Wait. Watch:** Begin with stillness. Do nothing but witness. Let the thoughts come. Let sensations pass. Don't interfere, just become aware of the movement of mind and feeling. This simple witnessing is the first key to opening the inner eye.

2. **Breathe Into Sensation**: Now bring your focus gently to the breath.
   - Feel the temperature of the air.
   - Feel how the breath moves through your nose, your throat, your chest.
   - Notice how it feels to be breathing *here, now*. Stay with the sensation of breath and let it anchor your attention.

3. **Recall with Gratitude**: Begin to envision, in rich detail, the people, places, animals, and memories you are most grateful for. See their faces. Feel their presence. Smell the air, taste the food, hear the voices. Let your senses participate in your memory. This is not nostalgia; it is

honoring your narrative. Your memories live within you, and by acknowledging them, you realign with your own story.

The more deeply you **immerse in gratitude**, the more you center yourself in a **state of happiness**. And that happiness is *fuel* for conscious creation.

4. **Enter the Timeless Point of Witness**: As you hold these visions and feelings, allow yourself to drop into the gap between past and future. It is not the outer world you are trying to experience; it is your **Self**.

As Heraclitus once said:

"No man ever steps in the same river twice, for it is not the same river and he is not the same man."

The present, as perceived by the senses, is always slightly delayed, processed milliseconds after the fact. But consciousness itself, the witness within, lives in *timeless presence*.

This is the activation of Ajna: to place your identity not in what you perceive, but in who is perceiving.

5. **Neutralize the Mental Oscillation**: The *Yoga Sutras* begin with this foundational truth:

योगस्चित्तवृत्तिनिरोध
"Yogaś citta-vṛtti-nirodhaḥ"

"Yoga is the cessation of the fluctuations of the mind."

-Patanjali.

Emotion is generated by contrast: pleasure and pain, hope and fear. But when you no longer identify with the waves, and instead root into the silent ocean beneath, you begin to master mental alchemy.

This is clarity. You can still feel, but you are not defined by what you feel. You become the clear sky, not the weather passing through it.

6. **Envision Fulfillment**: From this still point within, bring to mind the vision you expressed earlier: the desire, the goal, the future you long to create. Now feel it fulfilled.
   o What does it feel like once it's achieved?
   o Where do you feel it in your body?
   o What emotion rises when you know it's real?

FREQUENCY DESIGN: THE QUANTUM ART OF CREATION

In the AXIS system, this is the highest realm of creation: the mental-emotional frequency field, the quantum field of consciousness.

All of the chakras operate as fields. But Ajna tunes you to the field of causation, not effect.

In physics, the material world is a consequence of quantum events. Matter is the effect; vibration is the cause. So, if you wish to create change in the material world, you must first create change in the quantum field your thoughts, emotions, images, and inner alignment.

This is not just spiritual metaphor it is scientific reality. Studies in neuroscience show that visualization activates the same neural pathways as real physical activity. High-performance athletes, musicians, and creators use mental rehearsal to enhance performance.

For example, research from *Cleveland Clinic Foundation* found that people who only *imagined* doing bicep curls increased their muscle strength by 13.5% over several weeks, just by visualizing the motion!

This works because the brain doesn't distinguish much between real and vividly imagined experiences. So, by consciously designing what you envision, you are literally firing and wiring new neural pathways, shaping your mind and body to become what you see.

In this state, you don't chase your future. You become it.

सहस्रार

Sahasrara
(Crown Chakra)

The Crown and the Return to the Void

"There is no separation"

We are all consciousness, everything is one.

Sanskrit Name: सहस्रार (Sahasrāra)

Name Meaning: *Sahasrara* = "Thousand-Petaled"

Element: Void

Element (AXIS): Space / Void

Emotion: Destruction ↔ Creation

Location: Crown of the head

Color: Violet or White

Sound/Mantra: Silence or "Aum" (total vibration)

Musical Note: B

Nerve Center: Pineal gland

Primary Function: Union, transcendence, restoration

Body Systems: Brain cortex, pineal gland (adjacent), nervous system integration

THE PLACE OF REST AND RETURN

Sahasrara, the seventh chakra, is the culmination of the human energy system; the crown, the tip of the vertical axis, and the entry point into and from the unknown.

If Muladhara is the base of being, then Sahasrara is the portal to non-being. It is the portal to the **void**, the pure field of consciousness from which all things arise and to which all things return. This is not a void of emptiness in the negative sense, but a space of total potential, a quantum womb beyond individuality, beyond form, beyond desire.

At this level, the journey of identity dissolves. All the distinctions between self and other, between I and the world, between creator and created, begin to fade. This is the state of yoga in its deepest definition: **union**. In Sahasrara, the singularity of human awareness touches the infinite, or what mystics and scholars have called God, Source, or the Mind of the All.

This is the place of rest. The place where the psyche (often fragmented by activity, ambition, thought, and emotion) can dissolve into spaciousness. In the AXIS system, Sahasrara corresponds to the void state: the field, the space, the silence within and from which all vibrations arise.

It is outside the measurable spectrum, and yet, it holds the architecture of all possibility. Just as silence is not the absence of music but the space that allows it, the seventh chakra is not the absence of experience but the ground that restores, renews, and reimagines it.

THE CROWN OF CONSCIOUSNESS AND
THE DREAMER OF REALITY

Where Ajna offers vision and direction, Sahasrara offers release. This is the point at which the human antenna (anchored to the earth through the spine) reaches into the stars. It is the final gateway through which inspiration, illumination, and presence pour into the system. It does not need to be activated through effort, rather, it opens through surrender.

The Sahasrara chakra is not associated with a specific organ, because it governs the integration of the whole system. It is beyond identity. It is not something to be grasped, but something to be allowed. When it opens, the sense of self as a separate "I" gives way to the awareness of being *life itself*. Not as part of the dream, but as the dreamer itself.

To meditate at the crown is to allow stillness to engulf thought. To enter silence not for the absence of noise, but for the presence of vastness. The thousand petals of this chakra symbolize infinite channels of connection between you and the cosmos, between will and destiny, between soul and source.

In Sahasrara, there is no need to become anything. There is only the knowing that you already are. Not as a person, but as presence. As intelligence. As the witness, the dreamer, the pulse of creation.

THE SYSTEM OF EMOTIONAL PROCESSING

The Chakra System forms a dynamic chain through which all human emotions are experienced, transformed, and integrated. Each chakra holds a specific frequency of emotion, from the instinctual survival power and fears of Muladhara, to the boundless transcendence of Sahasrara.

Together, they allow the full spectrum of human experience to be processed, expressed, and elevated, ensuring that emotions are not just felt but channeled into action, growth, and higher awareness.

Without the proper alignment and awareness, the system can get overwhelmed, numbed or clogged. When aligned and consciously directed, they serve as the fuel for self-realization and authentic expression.

To understand the Chakras, we must understand they don't work separately, they aren't apart, isolated forces; they are different densities of the same energy field. The Chakra system is a map of the human vibrational spectrum of consciousness, manifesting from the subtle void, to tangible matter.

Although all Chakras work together and are part of one energy field, this energy can also be understood as seven different states of vibration. Just as the seven colors and the seven musical notes act as coordinates to a specific tone within the spectrum of vibration (whether in light or sound), each Chakras expresses a specific tone of emotional experience.

Each chakra holds the duality of experience: a spectrum of higher and lower expressions, where balance is found in conscious alignment.

Below is the full physical, psychological, and energetic description of each chakra, along with the Axis techniques that help activate and balance them.

THE CHAKRA SYSTEM

THE MECHANICS OF CONSCIOUSNESS AND THE PATH OF INNER ALCHEMY

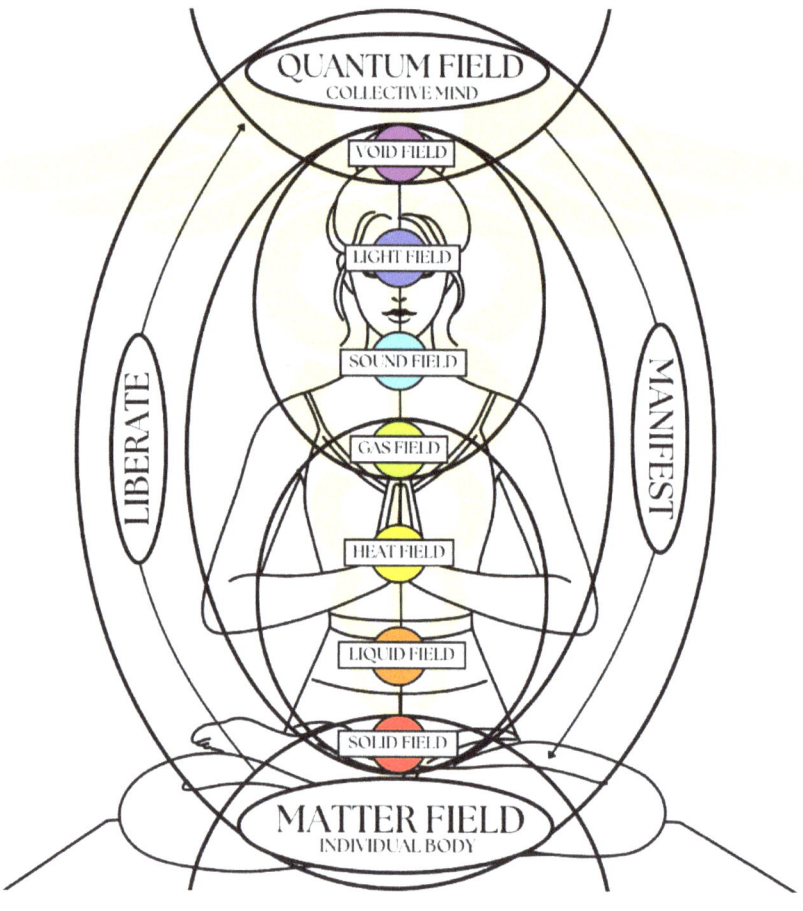

The chakra system is the living architecture of the human experience. It is the axis of the Self, the spine of consciousness through which all transformation flows. It is the pathway and mechanism for inner alchemy, self-mastery, and the basis of the Axis system.

Each chakra is a vibrational vortex, a layer in the spectrum of manifestation through which energy passes as it transforms, from pure potential into concrete form. This thermodynamic metamorphosis is not only energetic, but also deeply physical, emotional and psychological. It is the process through which Einstein equation $E = mc^2$ becomes embodied truth.

Einstein's theory for relativity tells us that **energy and matter are two sides of the same coin**, he understood that vibration, when slowed and condensed, becomes mass. This is the process that the chakra system governs. It is the internal ladder through which consciousness descends from the quantum world (the realm of imagination and non-local unity) into the physical realm of time, space, and form.

At the top of the axis, Sahasrara, the crown chakra, connects us to the mind of the All, the infinite void from which all ideas, images, and impulses arise. This is the field of imagination. From this Quantum source, vibration condenses as it flows downward through the seven chakras: through vision (Ajna), voice (Vishuddha), feeling (Anahata), will (Manipura), sensation (Svadhisthana), and finally structure (Muladhara). It is here (in the axis of the chakra system) that imagination becomes matter, tangible experience, this process is called the great art of manifestation.

In reverse, when energy rises from Muladhara, it becomes **healing**. The emotional residue of trauma stored in the tissues, held in posture, and buried in memory, can be elevated upward through each layer of self until it dissolves back into the Quantum Field. That which once anchored us in fear becomes light. This is the called **science of liberation**. The return to unity. The ascension of experience into wisdom.

This dynamic between **manifestation and liberation** is called the great art of **transmutation,** and it activates the full circuit of the Axis chakra system; allowing you to create and transform at will. This is the rhythm of the soul.

The Quantum Field is the realm of causes. The Matter Field is the realm of effects. And the chakra system is the spectrum which links them to create the human experience. Every act of creation is a descent, from idea to form. Every act of healing is an ascent, from matter, back to energy. Together, they weave **the path to the Self; a system for action that leads to conscious evolution.**

This is the purpose of the Axis system:

- To align the body, the breath, and the mind into one coherent flow.
- To transform your life from reaction to creation.
- To experience your being as a continuous field of self-awareness, expressing itself in many densities.
- To recognize that your thoughts shape your biology, your posture reveals your past, your voice carries your identity, and your desires; because if purified, can reshape your world.

When you live aligned with your axis, you become the artist of reality. You no longer merely exist and react; now you interact with it to shape it and inspire it. Your inner experience becomes art, and your art becomes a bridge into the imagination of others. This is how we participate in the collective dream and the evolution of the collective self. This is how we become one with THE ALL.

So, whether you are healing the past, or birthing the future, or both… remember:

Every transformation begins in the AXIS,

The AXIS is YOU.

THE CHAKRA SYSTEM:

THE SELF-REGULATORY BIOELECTRIC NETWORK

Recent studies in bio-electromagnetism suggest that the human body operates as a structured energy field, reinforcing the concept that chakras serve as points of bioelectrical convergence. Dr. Robert Becker's work on electrical properties of the nervous system demonstrated that bioelectrical signals govern tissue healing, stress responses, and cognitive processing (Becker & Selden, 1985).

Furthermore, research into biophotons (ultra-weak photon emissions from cells) suggests that living organisms communicate through bioelectrical and electromagnetic signaling (Popp, 1992). This supports the idea that chakra activation is a process of regulating bioelectrical charge, balancing energy distribution throughout the nervous and endocrine systems.

The chakra system, traditionally understood as a series of energy centers along the spinal column, correlates strongly with key neurological and endocrine structures in the body. According to Dr. Beverly Rubik, a leading researcher in biofield science, the human body generates electromagnetic activity that interacts with its physiological systems, forming a structured and layered biofield (Rubik, 2002).

Each chakra corresponds to a nerve plexus and a major endocrine gland, suggesting that these energy centers play a functional role in the regulation of physical, mental, and emotional states (Motoyama, 1981). Research into bio-electromagnetism has further demonstrated that each gland and neural network emits its own bioelectrical field, reinforcing the concept that the chakra system is a physiological reality manifesting through the body's electromagnetic activity (Becker & Selden, 1985).

THE HUMAN BIOELECTRICAL NETWORK.

Although traditional chakra theory describes seven distinct energy centers, modern neurophysiology suggests that these centers align with key components of the autonomic nervous system. Below are the scientific correlations between the chakra system and its physiological structures:

• Root Chakra – Solid field (Muladhara) → Pelvic Nerve Plexus & Adrenal Glands

The root chakra, associated with grounding, survival, and basic instincts, is linked to the pelvic nerve plexus and adrenal glands, which regulate the fight-or-flight stress response (Pert, 1999). The adrenal glands secrete cortisol and adrenaline, governing stress adaptation and survival mechanisms.

• Sacral Chakra – Liquid field (Swadhisthana) → Sacral Nerve Plexus & Reproductive Glands

This chakra regulates creativity, sexuality, and emotional processing, corresponding with the sacral nerve plexus, which controls reproductive function and emotional regulation through the hypothalamic-pituitary-gonadal (HPG) axis (McEwen, 2007).

• Solar Plexus Chakra – Heat field (Manipura) → Celiac Nerve Plexus & Digestive System

The solar plexus chakra is related to personal power and metabolic energy, aligning with the celiac nerve plexus, which influences digestive function and metabolic regulation through interactions with the gut-brain axis (Gershon, 1999).

• Heart Chakra – Gas field (Anahata) → Cardiac Nerve Plexus & Heart Electromagnetic Field

The heart chakra is the center of emotional processing and energetic balance, correlating with the cardiac nerve plexus and the heart's electromagnetic field. Research from the HeartMath Institute has shown that the heart generates the most powerful electromagnetic field in the body, influencing brain function, emotional regulation, and physiological coherence (McCraty et al., 2014).

• Throat Chakra – Sound field (Vishuddha) → Cervical Nerve Plexus & Thyroid Gland

The throat chakra, associated with communication and self-expression, corresponds with the cervical nerve plexus and thyroid gland, which regulates metabolic rate, vocal function, and neural activation (Guillemin & Rosenberg, 2004).

• Third Eye Chakra – Light field (Ajna) → Hypothalamus & Pineal Gland

This chakra governs intuition and cognitive perception, aligning with the pineal gland, which produces melatonin, affecting sleep cycles, neuroplasticity, and states of consciousness (Strassman, 2001).

• Crown Chakra – Void field (Sahasrara) → Prefrontal Cortex & Higher Brain Centers

The crown chakra, associated with higher consciousness, is linked to the prefrontal cortex, which regulates self-awareness, higher reasoning, and executive function (Davidson & McEwen, 2012).

THE SELF AND THE CHAKRAS

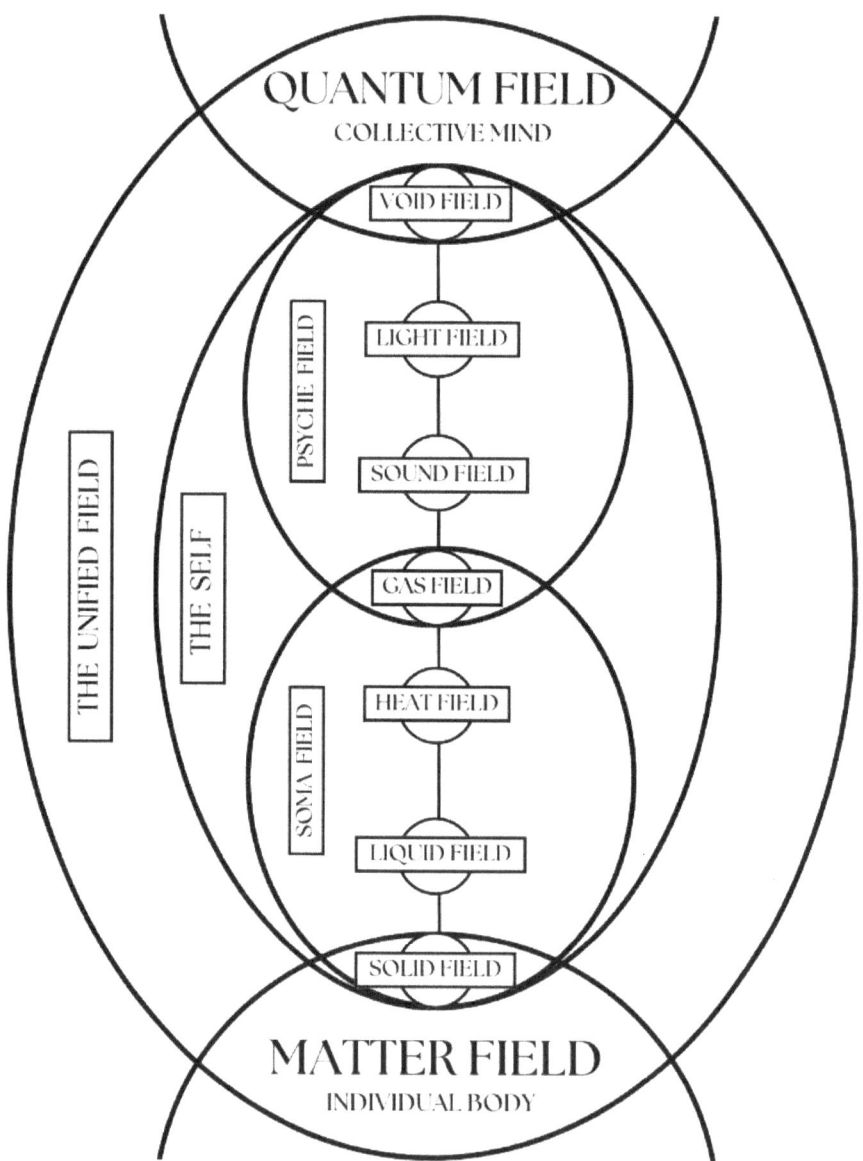

This graphic depicts the order and structure of the Self, the Soma, the Psyche, the Unified field, and all the 9 states of energy; from the Quantum, to the Matter.

The Axis System integrates the chakra system, long considered a spiritual and energetic framework, with modern neuroscience, endocrinology, and bio-electromagnetic research to create a practical model for self-regulation and peak performance. The three core elements of the Axis System (Postural alignment, conscious Breathwork, and focused Attention) are practiced in unison to activate, regulate, and optimize the energetic centers:

• Postural Alignment: Proper structural positioning ensures optimal nerve conductivity and energy distribution across the spine, where chakras are located. Studies show that spinal alignment directly influences Vagus nerve function, which regulates stress, digestion, and cardiovascular health (Porges, 2011).

• Breathwork Regulation: Controlled breathing techniques alter autonomic nervous system balance, influencing heart coherence and neural oscillations. Research demonstrates that rhythmic breathwork increases parasympathetic activity, reducing stress and enhancing brain-heart coherence (Jerath et al., 2006).

• Focused Attention: Meditation and visualization practices regulate neural plasticity and endocrine function, reinforcing cognitive flexibility and emotional resilience (Lutz et al., 2008).

Scientific studies confirm that electromagnetic and bioelectric processes regulate cellular activity, stress adaptation, and cognitive function, reinforcing the validity of ancient chakra-based practices. By merging ancient wisdom with modern scientific methodologies, the Axis System provides a comprehensive model for human evolution and self-mastery.

STRUCTURE OF THE UNIFIED SELF.

At the core of mastering the energy field is the understanding that being, feeling, and perceiving are not separate functions, they are aspects of the same unified force. These three fields of existence (the body, the emotions, and the mind, or the Soma, the Psyche and the Psychosomatic experience A.k.a: "the Self") are not independent; they are woven together within the electromagnetic framework of the human energy system. This integration of the Self is not theoretical; it is structural, functional, and deeply experiential.

The Chakra system is the architecture of this integration. It is the map of experience itself (the mechanism through which we process life, transform energy, and express consciousness). The seven chakras do not simply exist as separate points along the spine; they represent the way energy moves through us, the way we intake and express experience.

To fully integrate the Axis System, we must understand how the chakras function as the meeting point of two primary forces:

1. The descending force, **Gravity**: the energy that governs over the Soma, the body, and the structure of experience.

   - This is the force of being, the three lower chakras, responsible for the survival, the senses, and the will power.
   - It is Quantum consciousness becoming biological Matter.

2. The ascending force, **Will**: the energy of the Psyche, the mind, radiation, and awareness.

   - This is the force of perceiving, the three upper chakras, responsible for expression, insight, and transcendence.
   - It is Matter and sensations becoming consciousness, concepts, ideas, language

The Breath (Prana, life force) is the bridge between these two realms. It is the connector, the intermediary, the flow that unifies both worlds. The moment breath becomes conscious, intentional, and harmonized with posture and attention, it activates the entire system, weaving together the forces of body and mind into a single, coherent field.

THE VORTEX OF INTEGRATION

The fourth chakra, Anahata, is the axis upon which the entire human experience revolves. The heart chakra bridges both worlds; it is the emotional body, the gateway through which all experience is felt, processed, and ultimately transformed.

This is why feeling is the bridge. It is not separate from thought, nor separate from the body; it is the unifying thread that weaves perception and being into one continuous flow of experience.

To feel is to integrate. The mind perceives, the body acts, but the feeling is the experience itself.

AWAKENING:

THE ACTIVATION OF THE SYSTEM

When we activate the Axis System, we are not just working with breath, posture, and attention separately; we are bringing them into full coherence within the electromagnetic structure of the chakras.

When these three forces come together within the chakra system, the body no longer feels separate from the mind, and the mind no longer feels separate from the body. The Self is experienced as one continuous electromagnetic field, a vortex of movement, energy, and perception.

This is the awakening of the holistic Self.

This is the shift from fragmented experience to total coherence.

This is the true purpose of the Axis System: not just to master the body, breath, and mind as separate entities, but to master the unified Self as an electromagnetic, self-organizing field of consciousness and the operational system of human experience.

This is the Self-Realized being.

This is the Awakened Human.

THE GATEWAY TO PRATYAHARA

As we explore the chakras as the energetic structure of experience, we come to a profound realization: the senses are not separate, they are different gateways to perceive the one and only nature of reality. The human body perceives reality through five primary senses (sight, sound, touch, taste, and smell), but in truth, these are simply different ways of detecting and understanding the same underlying field of vibration.

The integration of our senses allows us to create a sense of reality that is not only based on the apparent and superficial shape, form, size and color; but rather based in vibration, and the frequency of its force.

When we understand that everything is energy, we begin to perceive all matter, emotion, and thought as a dynamic field; we start to see beyond the limited capacity of our senses and into the interconnected nature of all waves. Light is a wave. Sound is a wave. Temperature is a wave. Each of these is merely a different frequency within the same sea of reality, and once we grasp this, we move beyond isolated sensory perception into a unified state of awareness.

This state is known as Pratyahara: The integration of the senses. In this state, we no longer perceive sight, sound, and touch as separate experiences, but rather as unified field of vibration. We are no longer confined to only seeing what is in front of us, hearing what is within range, or feeling only through direct contact. When we awaken the unified sense of Pratyahara, we expand our perception for it to become more sensitive, more accurate, wider in its reach, and an all-immersive spherical awareness.

When this occurs, we unlock a broader field of awareness, allowing us to perceive what is usually unseen. Not because we are developing some supernatural power, but because we are removing the illusion of separation between sensory experience. Through this heightened state, we begin to perceive subtle energies like the emotional fields of others, the residual energy in spaces, the vibrational signature of thoughts, the living aura of beings, the presence of entities and many more vibrational qualities of the reality we are in.

CHAPTER XI

NURTURING THE AXIS

Alignment is not enough. One may stand perfectly aligned along the axis (spine upright, breath organized, awareness centered) and yet feel depleted, fragile, or unable to sustain power. This is because alignment governs the energy distribution, while nutrition governs energy availability.

The Axis System is built upon two inseparable pillars of well-being:

> 1.   Alignment of the axis: the capacity to organize energy efficiently along the central channel of the self.

> 2.   Nurturing of the Self: the continuous replenishment of the system across all of its fields.

Without nourishment, alignment becomes sterile.

Without alignment, nourishment becomes chaotic.

True vitality arises when a well-aligned axis is continuously fed by high-quality inputs across every dimension of being.

Nutrition in the Axis understanding is not limited to food. Nutrition is anything that enters the system and contributes to coherence, regeneration, and power. To nourish the human being fully, we must feed each of the seven fundamental fields through which consciousness expresses itself.

THE SEVEN FIELDS OF NUTRITION

1. The Solid Field: Nourishment Through Food.

The solid field corresponds to the densest expression of matter: bones, muscles, organs, connective tissue. It is the foundation upon which all higher fields rest.

This field is nourished through solid food, but not merely through calories or macronutrients. The body responds to quality, coherence, and familiarity.

High-quality nutrition for the solid field includes:

- Whole, unprocessed foods.
- Ingredients grown in living soil.
- Foods your ancestry and genetics are adapted to digest.
- Meals prepared with attention, care, and respect.

The body recognizes food that comes from a coherent ecosystem. When the solid field is nourished properly, the body feels grounded, stable, and resilient. Artificial low-quality food creates noise in the system, stealing energy from the axis instead of supplying it.

The rule is simple:

Eat food that feels like it belongs to your body.

2. The Liquid Field: Nourishment Through Hydration.

The liquid field governs blood, lymph, synovial fluid, and cellular hydration. It is responsible for the transportation of nutrients into the tissues and cells, as well as the cleansing of toxins, and the inmune's system adaptability to threats and pathogens.

This field is nourished through liquids, primarily water — but not all water is equal.

Optimal nourishment of the liquid field includes:

- Clean, mineral-rich water.
- Natural electrolytes (sodium, potassium, magnesium).
- Herbal infusions and broths.

Hydration is not about quantity alone; it is about absorbability. When the liquid field is nourished, the body flows with ease, joints feel free, emotions move without stagnation, and energy circulates smoothly along the axis.

3. The Heat Field: Nourishment Through Action.

Heat is life. Without internal fire, digestion weakens, immunity drops, motivation fades, and consciousness dulls. The heat field is nourished primarily through movement and exertion.

This includes:

- Strength training.

- Dynamic movement.

- Cardiovascular exercise.

- Any practice that raises internal temperature with intention.

Exercise is not merely mechanical — it is a ritual of awakening inner power. Through movement, we stoke the fire that allows transformation to occur. A nourished heat field produces confidence, vitality, and the ability to act decisively in the world.

Without fire, alignment becomes passive. With fire, alignment becomes force.

4. The Gas Field: Nourishment Through Breath.

The gas field corresponds to respiration, oxygenation, and subtle gaseous exchange. Breath is the interface between matter and consciousness.

This field is nourished through:

- Conscious breathing practices.

- Exposure to clean, unpolluted air.

- Time spent in nature.

- Steam therapies.

Breathing high-quality air is increasingly rare—and therefore increasingly valuable. Forests, oceans, mountains, and open natural spaces provide a density of life-supporting gases that no indoor environment can replicate.

Additionally, herbal steam therapy introduces therapeutic gases that support detoxification, circulation, and nervous system regulation.

5. The Sound Field: Nourishment Through Vibration.

Sound organizes matter. Cells respond to frequency before they respond to chemistry.

The sound field is nourished through:

- Music that resonates with your state of mood and vibration.

- Natural sounds (wind, water, silence between sounds).

- Singing, chanting, and vocal expression.

- Speech that is truthful and coherent.

Sound can either harmonize or fragment the system. Nourishing the sound field restores rhythm to the axis and clarity to the mind. A well-fed sound field sharpens intuition, emotional intelligence, and relational attunement.

6. The Light Field: Nourishment Through Sunlight.

Light governs circadian rhythm, hormonal balance, mood, and perception. It is one of the most neglected yet essential nutrients of modern life.

The light field is nourished through:

- Direct exposure to natural sunlight.
- Morning and late-afternoon sun when possible.

Thought sunlight is not actually a nutrient, it is an essential component in the synthetization of Vitamin D; this vitamin is essential for bone health, immune function, and many other bodily processes. It regulates mental health, energy cycles, and cellular communication. When the light field is deprived, the axis weakens regardless of alignment.

A nourished light field restores clarity, optimism, and temporal harmony.

7. The Void Field: Nourishment Through Silence.

Beyond all fields lies the void; the field of rest, dissolution, and infinite potential.

The void field is nourished through:

- Silence
- Stillness
- Resting attention beyond thought and identity

This nourishment does not add energy, it restores coherence. By returning regularly to the void beyond space and time, the nervous system resets; consciousness releases its burdens, and the axis re-centers effortlessly. This is where power regenerates itself.

INTEGRATION:

POWER THROUGH COHERENCE

When all seven fields are nourished, a direct relationship emerges between the material body and the quantum field of consciousness. Energy flows freely, perception sharpens, and the axis gains power to produce intention.

No matter how perfectly aligned the axis may be, a neglected system cannot hold power.

True vitality is the result of:

- Alignment.
- Nourishment.
- Coherence.

This is how the electromagnetic field of a human being becomes stable, radiant, and strong—not through force, but through intelligent care.

To nourish yourself is ESSENTIAL.

It is the discipline that provides you the power to build the life you deserve.

CHAPTER XII
THE EXPANSION OF PERCEPTION

THE PATH OF THE MYSTIC

Before we embark on this journey, a warning must be given. The expansion of perception is a gift, but it is also a responsibility. Those who begin to perceive beyond the limitations of ordinary awareness will find themselves in a vast and limitless ocean of possibility. While this can be profoundly enlightening, it can also be overwhelming, confusing, and even destabilizing as you get used to the immensity of the experience.

When perception expands, it does not do so in a controlled, step-by-step manner. It is more like a floodgate opening, revealing an endless flow of information. Those who do not know how to regulate their energy, how to ground themselves, or how to navigate this expanded state may find themselves spinning out of control, unable to make sense of the influx of new sensations, emotions, and insights.

This is why patience and regulation are essential. There is no rush in the path of awakening. Your ability to process information is the true limitation, not the information itself. Just as a child must first learn to walk before, they can run, so too must you develop the capacity to handle expanded awareness before diving into its depths.

This chapter will serve as a guide to stabilizing the expansion of perception, ensuring that as your awareness grows, it does so in a way that is grounded, integrated, and empowering, rather than chaotic and overwhelming.

THE GIFT AND THE DANGER OF EXPANDED PERCEPTION

To perceive beyond the physical realm is to enter the mystic state. This is a state in which the lines between thought, energy, and experience blur, allowing for direct interaction with the unseen forces of existence.

As you begin to sense the emotions of others as clearly as you once heard their words, feeling energy moving through places, receive thoughts not only from your own mind but from the larger field of consciousness, a new world opens up.

This can lead to:

- A heightened ability to understand people and their emotions.
- The capacity to sense stagnant or vibrant energies in spaces.
- A stronger intuitive sense (knowing things before they happen).

However, without guidance, this can also lead to:

- Mental noise: So much information that it becomes difficult to focus.
- Emotional instability: Feeling too much, too deeply and without proper processing.
- Spiritual delusion: Misinterpreting subtle experiences as absolute truths.

- Anxiety or paranoia: Perceiving things without a structured framework to understand them.
- If unattended, this can lead to schizophrenic states of perception.

For this reason, it is crucial to not only open perception, but to learn how to regulate, refine, and navigate it with wisdom and patience.

THE PATH THROUGH SAMSARA AND INTO NIRVANA

In many mystical traditions, there is a term known as Samsara: the endless cycle of experience, creation, and the looping experience of regular human perception. Those who unlock their perception, enter a state where infinite possibilities, stories, and realms of experience unfold.

This is a beautiful and powerful state, but it can also lead to exhaustion, confusion, and entrapment within the cycle of endless creation. The mystic who expands perception too quickly finds themselves drawn into a never-ending sea of experience, a place where one can create and manifest endlessly, but without direction or clarity.

This is why the path must lead beyond Samsara and into Nirvana. Nirvana is not an external place, it is the state of peace within experience, the ability to remain centered even as the waves of infinite possibilities crash around you.

In other words, the goal is not simply to see more, feel more, and experience more; it is to learn how to rest in the center of all experience, moving through life with clarity, power, and peace.

This is why moral and ethical codes become essential. Without guiding principles, expanded perception can lead to manipulation, distortion, and loss of clarity. Those who awaken their perception but lack discipline risk falling into illusions of power, personal delusions, and the chaos of unstructured awareness.

To navigate this path, we must return to the ancient wisdom of the Yamas and Niyamas (the Ethical and Moral codes of the yogic tradition). These principles act as anchors for expanded perception, ensuring that as we awaken to greater levels of reality, we remain clear, balanced, and aligned with the highest purpose.

THE MYSTIC'S RESPONSIBILITY

You are now a mystic. As you begin to awaken your perception, as you start to work with energy, as you activate the deeper layers of your consciousness, it is vital to recognize that there are laws.

These are not laws in the sense of restrictions, nor commandments designed to bind you. They are the natural principles that govern reality (the seven Hermetic Laws) the universal forces that shape the movement of energy. And beyond them, there is wisdom that has been left to us by the great sages of the past, guides who have walked this path long before us and understood the power that comes with awakening.

One of the greatest of these sages was Patanjali, the mystic yogi who left us the Yoga Sutras, the foundational text that underlies much of what we have explored in this book. Patanjali did not merely teach techniques, he taught a way of being, a way of moving through the world with integrity and wisdom. He understood that the power of expanded perception is not just about what one can do, but about how one wields that power.

In his teachings, he outlined ten principles: the Yamas and Niyamas. This are not about rigid rules or prohibitions, but qualities of nature, forces to align with, rather than resist. These principles are here to guide your energy, to refine your actions, and to ensure that your power is expressed in its most graceful and potent way.

THE NIYAMAS

नियमा

THE CODE AND CYCLE OF MANIFESTATION

Everything in existence moves through cycles. From the breath to biological rhythms, from thought patterns to planetary motion; life is fundamentally wave-based. This applies not only to nature, but to manifestation itself. In the AXIS system, the entire purpose of aligning posture, breath, and attention is to act consciously and in coherence with the laws of nature, to move in rhythm with causality rather than against it, and to participate skillfully in the process of shaping reality through aligned action.

This is why the Niyamas are not just internal virtues or ancient disciplines, they are a behavioral code to achieve your highest goals. More than a path of personal development, the Niyamas are a blueprint for turning "Karma" (the automatic, unconscious patterns and lineage of cause and effect) into "Dharma" (the conscious creation of action and consequence through decision and flow).

In Karma, the outcome shapes the Self.

In Dharma, the Self shapes the outcome.

These principles are not new. They were structured thousands of years ago by the Brahmanic sages of the Indus Valley, who composed the **Vedas**, the root texts of the entire yoga tradition. These mystics were not only priests but scientists of consciousness, who understood that reality (what they called *Maya*) is not an illusion, but a structured field of vibrational causality. They knew that any act of true creation required first an internal alignment. What they encoded in the Niyamas was not dogma, but a technical system for influencing the matrix of cause and effect.

This system was created to break through our limited state of programmed and unconscious behavior (Karma) and tap into our authentic expression; the one which creates and manifests our desired experience.

This entire process of becoming can be summarized as a five-step process: Purification, Attunement, Alignment, Reflection and Release.

This is the inner architecture for conscious manifestation. It is what turns action into art, discipline into presence, and motion into manifestation. When lived fully, the Niyamas shift your state of being into one that naturally attracts higher realities. You no longer chase outcomes; you become a resonance through which outcomes emerge. This is not mystical thinking; it is vibrational physics.

SHAUCHA

शौच

The Discipline of Purification

Shaucha, the first of the Niyamas, is the principle of **purity**. Not just in the external sense, but as an active, intentional cleansing of the inner world. In the AXIS system, Shaucha is understood as the conscious removal of toxicity (either physical, mental, emotional, or energetic) so that the system can return to its natural rhythm and coherence. It is not about appearing clean; it is about becoming clear *through purification*.

True purity begins with the Psyche. What stories are you carrying? What assumptions, judgments, or inherited beliefs cloud your perception? The mind can become polluted just as the body; by repetitive and obsessive thoughts, by unresolved trauma, by the narratives that shape Self-image. Shaucha asks for purification of Mind: not silence, but refinement. Not perfection, but honesty. It is the discipline of observing what does not belong and releasing it before it takes root.

In the Soma, the purification process must also be active. Shaucha governs the clarity of the digestive system, the organs of elimination, and all metabolic processes that convert experience (nutritional or emotional) into energy. When the physical body is burdened with excess, stagnation, or inflammation, the mind suffers. Just as waste must exit the body, impressions and emotional residues must be metabolized and cleared. Without this internal hygiene, no transformation can take place.

This is why Shaucha applies to all layers of the Self:

- **Purity of sensation**: Refining sensory input through rest, silence, and intentional environments.

- **Purity of narrative**: Letting go of distorted stories we tell ourselves about who we are.

- **Purity of relationship**: Recognizing when interactions reinforce toxicity instead of truth.

- **Purity of space**: Maintaining environments that support stillness and health.

- **Purity of attention**: Choosing what you watch, read, listen to, and consume with awareness.

Shaucha is a ritual of realignment. It is not something we achieve once, but a daily act of restoration. The body is purified through sweat, water, breath, and food. The psyche is purified through reflection, truthfulness, and release. The spirit is purified through devotion and simplicity.

In AXIS, Shaucha is the foundational **act of returning** to the original signal, the untangled frequency of Self, your authentic signature of vibration. Purity is not repression or control. It is the power to create space for what is sacred. Without that space, no higher awareness, no integrated expression, can move through.

SANTOSHA

सन्तोष

The Discipline of Gratitude

Santosha, the second Niyama, is the cultivation of **satisfaction**. Not just the neutral acceptance of contentment, but the embodied joy of being deeply nourished by what already is. In the AXIS system, Santosha is understood as the discipline of gratitude: the conscious practice of tuning the system to recognize fullness, presence, and the sufficiency of the now. This is not about settling; it is about creating the internal conditions for expansion.

Satisfaction is a living frequency. It's the moment where you exhale and feel, *"This is enough. I am enough."* From that space (not of craving but of trust) you become receptive, your field stabilizes, your vibration rises. That subtle shift magnetizes the next experience into your life; one that resonates with the joy you're already carrying.

Unlike neutral contentment, satisfaction carries a positive charge, it's energized. It creates a sense of *readiness*, an eager openness to what comes next. Not because you're escaping the now, but because you've anchored yourself so deeply in it that the future becomes an extension of your joy, instead of an escape from your lack.

This inner state directly affects how energy moves through your system. The more satisfied your nervous system feels, the more creative, fluid, and stable your field becomes. Santosha is therefore the baseline frequency from which sustainable creation begins. Without it, desire becomes tension. With it, desire becomes magnetism.

Practicing Santosha might look like:

- Feeling the fullness of your breath before reaching for the next thing.

- Reframing challenges as teachers and transitions as gifts.

- Relishing the small things as if they were already the answer.

- Shifting the inner question from "What's missing?" to "What's already here?"

In this state gratitude becomes the seed. Satisfaction becomes the soil. And from that resonance, the future blooms filled with reasons to be grateful for.

You move forward not because you lack, but because you're lit from within. You create not to prove yourself, but to expand the fullness you already feel.

Satisfaction is the sacred pause that lets you sync with the intelligence of life.

Gratitude is the signal that tells the universe:

I'm aligned.

I'm available.

Show me what's next!

TAPAS

तपस्

The Discipline of the Self

Tapas, the third Niyama, is the discipline of **self-generated fire**: the sacred heat that transforms potential into power. In the AXIS system, Tapas is not about deprivation or punishment. It is the **pressure that aligns**. The deliberate, conscious intensity that presses the system closer to its axis, refining its vibration, strengthening its coherence, and expanding its vertical range.

At the most subtle level, every part of your being is vibrating. Your cells, thoughts, breath, and attention all oscillate. Without direction, that motion becomes scattered. Tapas is the inner force that contracts motion towards the center, drawing all oscillations into alignment with the spine (the electromagnetic core of consciousness). Remember that as the system contracts horizontally, it expands vertically. The self becomes a more precise antenna, able to receive gravity and transmit radiation.

This is not a metaphor; it is the energetic mechanics of the Self. The more pressure the system can hold, the more radiant it becomes. The stronger the gravitational field you can tolerate (through resisting distraction, inertia, and compulsion) the more light you can generate. Just as stars form through compression, the self becomes luminous through **self-discipline**. This aligns with one of the foundational principles in Kabbalah: *resistance to compulsion creates lasting light*.

Tapas is the practice of that law. It is the price of becoming what you envision by resisting what tempts you away from it.

To live Tapas is to honor the pressure as a sacred price in the process of becoming the sacred diamond which represents the purest and most powerful expression of your Self.

This is the gateway to Self-Realization. This is where your truly test and challenge your identity, sensations and power of will to create freely. And this is the highest form of discipline.

Tapas is the fire that:

- Refines posture and behavior until they resonate with integrity.

- Focuses the mind through purpose and choice.

- Turns discomfort into evolution.

- Pulls the system into alignment so it can rise with clarity and force.

Tapas is not effort for its own sake, it is **devotion** to the self you are becoming. It is the conscious friction that sculpts identity. When practiced fully, it activates the entire electromagnetic field, expanding consciousness.

In the end, Tapas is not about force. It is about honoring your will, your axis, and the vision that called you forward. It is the discipline of the self, for the realization of the Self.

SVADHYAYA

स्वाध्याय

The Science of Self-Study

Svadhyaya, the fourth Niyama, translates to *self-study*, but in the AXIS system, it is more accurately described as the science of self-observation. It is the practice of studying the self not through opinion, but through presence. Not to judge, but to understand. Svadhyaya is how you come to know the patterns that shape you, the programs that drive you, and the deeper Self that witnesses them all.

This is the art of tracking how your system behaves across time, how your breath changes under stress, how your posture adapts in different social settings, and how your desires are shaped by mood or memory.

Svadhyaya is the discipline of reading yourself as a field, noticing the waves of thought and the architecture of emotion, and to decode what they reveal about your inner alignment.

In the AXIS framework, Svadhyaya is the mirror of consciousness. It is what allows the Self to become aware of its motion. Without this reflective capacity, we remain trapped within reactive cycles, with it, we gain the ability to respond with intelligence rather than habit. Observation creates choice and repeated observation creates transformation.

This Niyama is the bridge between discipline and wisdom. If Tapas is the fire, Svadhyaya is the awareness that witnesses what the fire reveals. It teaches you how to sit with yourself, even when you are uncomfortable, it cultivates intimacy with your own mind; not to tame it, but to understand its design.

Practicing Svadhyaya means:

- Journaling your triggers, cravings, or repeating emotional patterns.

- Tracking your breath, posture, and internal state throughout the day.

- Studying sacred texts or spiritual teachings, not to memorize but to mirror.

- Observing the "inner narrator" without letting it define you.

- Asking, *Who is the one aware of this thought?*

Ultimately, Svadhyaya leads to freedom; not because it changes who you are, but because it reveals the true nature of yourself. The axis becomes conscious, and from that place of inner knowing, all possible actions become rooted in truth.

ISHVARAPRANIDHANA

ईश्वरप्रणिधान

The Surrender to the Source

Ishvarapranidhana, the fifth and final Niyama, is often translated as *surrender to God*, yet in the Axis system, it is understood as the surrender to Source, to the greater intelligence that animates existence. It is not the abandonment of will, but the recognition that there is a deeper will moving through all things, and that our highest alignment comes when we offer our efforts to that current, rather than trying to dominate it.

This is the Niyama of humility and trust. Where Tapas demands effort, and Svadhyaya demands insight, Ishvarapranidhana invites **release**. It teaches that after discipline and self-study, there must be devotion. That after clarity and refinement, we must let go! Not in defeat, but in reverence. It is the practice of not clinging to outcomes, to identities, to the illusion of control.

In the Axis framework, Ishvarapranidhana is the final integration point where the self-realigns with the field of consciousness itself. The system becomes tuned, vibrant, ready, and then it opens; it blooms.

This surrender is not passive. It is a conscious act of alignment with the unknown. It is what allows synchronicity, insight, and transformation to arrive without being forced. When you've done the work and let go of the outcome, you become an instrument for a greater design.

Practicing Ishvarapranidhana might mean:

- Letting go of timelines and trusting the mystery in the process.

- Offering your work, practice, or path to something beyond ego.

- Releasing the need to always "figure it out".

- Bowing to what is, especially when it's not what you expected.

- Meditating not to master the mind, but to become receptive to the consciousness of creation.

This Niyama teaches that you are not alone in the unfolding. There is a rhythm behind the rhythm, a pulse beneath your pulse. And when you surrender to it, you access a grace that effort alone cannot produce.

In the deepest sense, Ishvarapranidhana is the remembrance that life is not yours to control, but it is yours to join. And when you do, your personal axis becomes attuned to the axis of the universe. You don't just move; you are moved.

THE YAMAS

यमा

THE CODE OF RADIANT PRESENCE

Where the Niyamas offer the foundation for inner success, the Yamas reveal the codes for outer success. The architecture of how to stand in the world with integrity, clarity, and power. Together, they form the two wings of the same bird, without one, the other cannot fly.

The Yamas are not rules. They are not constraints. They are principles of vibrational alignment that allow your inner axis to harmonize with the external world. Each one is a declaration of personal sovereignty. An affirmation of the subtle yet unshakable force of one who lives in conscious relationship with reality.

AHIMSA

अहिंसा

The Power of Kindness

Ahimsa is often translated as "non-violence," but this translation misses its subtle brilliance. Violence is only the final echo in a long sequence of reactions; the true target of Ahimsa is much earlier in the chain. Ahimsa is not the suppression of violence, it is the prevention of friction, the force that dissolves friction before it causes harm.

Friction is the first energetic rupture between particles, between people and between selves, it creates heat, that heat generates pain, and pain leads to conflict. When hardened and fed, this conflict gives rise to violence, and violence (be it emotional, psychological, or physical) leaves behind wounds that ripple forward in time, becoming the trauma passed down through families, generations, and civilizations.

Kindness is the first real expression of power and sovereignty in relationship. It is not weakness, is not compliance; it is the capacity to hold yourself so deeply that you no longer react from your wounds. It is the strength to interrupt cycles that have traveled through time and blood, and to say: *this pain ends with me*.

When we practice kindness in the face of potential friction, we break the karmic loop. We do not pass on what was passed down. We relate, rather than react.

We widen the field, we soften the edge, and in that moment, something new becomes possible: a different outcome, a different experience, a different future.

Kindness, when practiced consistently, generates a new wave of causality. It becomes a new field of frequency, one that others can feel. It opens the door to trust, and with trust, the collective begins to heal. We start to see each other not as threats or strangers, but as fellow travelers in a shared mystery. As Baba Ram Dass said, *"We are all just walking each other home"*, kindness is the path beneath our feet.

This doesn't mean we avoid difficult conversations or bypass the truth. It means we carry our truth with gentleness. We offer our perspective without needing to crush another's. We learn to meet each being as a unique antenna; each tuned to their own vibration of experience. We begin to understand that everyone's reality is valid and truth in some way (even if it contradicts our own).

As the *Kybalion* teaches: *"All truths are but half-truths."* Your truth is true within the lens of your perception! Everyone is filtering consciousness through their own nervous system, language, memory, culture, and trauma. The human experience is a multiverse; kindness is what allows these different universes to coexist.

When we recognize this, we stop needing to be "right." We begin to honor truth as relational rather than absolute, this is perhaps the highest function of Ahimsa: to make space for other people's experience without needing to dominate or erase it. Kindness does this. It bridges perception with care, it transforms opposition into connection; and in doing so, it becomes a revolutionary force of transmutation.

In the AXIS system, Ahimsa is not merely a moral rule; it is a technology of coherence. It calibrates your field so that your presence does not produce harm, but resonance. It is the intelligence that prevents breakdown by allowing flow. The energetic alignment that ensures your system meets others not with sharpness, but with stability and warmth.

Kindness doesn't mean you'll never feel anger or hurt. But it does mean you become conscious of how you move with it.

You pause. You breathe. You take responsibility. You act from the center, not from the wound.

When you do this over and over again; you become the kind of person whose energy liberates others, whose gentleness disarms fear, whose steadiness dissolves tension. You become a tuning fork for peace, a living example of what it looks like when trauma is not inherited but transformed.

This is the power of Ahimsa. This is the **power of kindness**. It doesn't just stop violence; it rewrites the field through presence. It creates trust, it restores dignity; and it allows us, together, to take one step closer to home.

SATYA

सत्य

The Power of Truth

Satya is often translated as "truthfulness," but in the AXIS system, it reveals itself as something much more profound: the direct pathway to sovereignty. It is the force that synchronizes your inner and outer worlds, and that synchronization is the beginning of true power. Truth, in this sense, is not just about factual correctness, it is about the alignment between what you know, what you say, what you do, and ultimately: who you are.

Satya is the foundation of authorship. What you are experiencing, is a direct consequence of your will.

Your perception is shaped by your vibration, and your vibration is the sum of your choices, your posture, your breath, your attention.

Even when circumstances appear to come from outside, the environment is not separate from you. You are not merely influenced by your environment; you are a part of it.

The *Kybalion* teaches: *"The All is Mind."* This means the universe is mental. Reality unfolds in response to intention, and intention is shaped by belief. Your truth is the engine of your belief system. How you perceive determines what you create.

This is the power of Satya: to realize that the stories you repeat to yourself, the values you choose to honor, the limits you accept or reject, all have the weight of the Law. Satya demands strength to live truthfully to take radical responsibility, not only for your words and actions, but for the entire narrative architecture of your life.

You must ask: *What do I really believe? What am I pretending not to know? What part of me have I silenced to avoid disruption?* Truth is not always comfortable, but it is always liberating.

When you speak your truth – fully, responsibly, clearly – you calibrate your system. Your axis becomes coherent, and in that coherence, confidence arises, not as performance, but as presence. You are no longer hiding anything, you are no longer split; the mind, the body, the voice, and the field are unified in a single frequency. That frequency is your signature vibration, and it is this signature that gives you power in the world.

Satya, then, is the practice of becoming **an artist of reality**. You are sculpting your timeline. You are making vows to yourself and honoring them with action. This is what it means to live in sovereignty: to speak a truth so aligned with your being that reality adjusts to accommodate it.

Truth creates integrity, integrity creates confidence, confidence allows connection, and connection gives birth to creation. In this sense, Satya is not a restriction; it is a liberation. It is the frequency that allows you to become a conscious participant in your own becoming.

This is the power of truth. It does not require external permission; it requires internal precision. The moment you align with it fully…you become a **radiant force**! A coherent field, a sovereign being walking in authenticity, with the world responding accordingly.

ASTEYA

अस्तेय

The Power of Integrity

Asteya is often translated as "non-stealing," but this superficial translation misses the deep energetic truth it points toward. In the Axis system, we do not speak in terms of good or bad, right or wrong. We speak in terms of cause and effect, of vibrational resonance and energetic coherence. When seen through this lens, Asteya reveals itself not as a rule of morality, but as a law of energetic alignment: the law of integrity.

To steal is not merely to take something that doesn't belong to you. It is to take on the karma of someone else; to absorb the fruit of a journey you haven't walked, the consequence of an action you haven't earned, the vibration of a path you haven't lived. It is to insert into your field an outcome that is not the effect of your own becoming, this creates disorder.

In the Axis framework, your life experience is the natural outcome of your state of vibration (the integration of your thoughts, posture, breath, attention, desires, decisions and sensations). Whatever comes to you is not random; it is equivalent to what you are. To take what hasn't come through you is to disrupt the law of equivalence. It is to put an effect into the field without the matching cause, and the result is incoherence.

This is why so many people who receive sudden wealth end up losing it. If the field hasn't been prepared, if the self hasn't expanded to hold the frequency of that abundance, the energy collapses. The person hasn't become what's required to sustain the experience. The vibration isn't there, and without that vibration, there is no stability; only burden, confusion, or loss.

Asteya teaches that you can only truly keep what you have become. When you become what you truly wish to have, it will flow to you as a natural outcome of your frequency. This is what integrity means in the deepest sense: coherence between being, feeling, doing and having.

To practice Asteya is to reject shortcuts that bypass your process. It is to trust that the life meant for you will come through you when you've aligned with its requirements. It is to stop reaching outward for what others have, and instead reach inward toward what you must become.

Asteya becomes the power of integrity: the principle that nothing truly belongs to you unless it was born through your vibration. When you violate this, you don't just take from another, you compromise yourself. You overload your system with foreign frequencies. You delay your own becoming by trying to substitute process with possession.

When you honor Asteya, you build something far more valuable than acquisition: you build self-authorship. You become someone who can be trusted with power, wealth, and responsibility because your field is clear, earned, **real**. From that clarity, you don't need to chase what others have, you magnetize what matches your essence.

Asteya reminds us: you are always becoming. Everything you need is available, but it must come through you. You cannot steal the harvest of a field you didn't till, but if you till your field with discipline, presence, and truth, the harvest will come in absolute coherence. It always does.

BRAHMACHARYA

ब्रह्मचर्य

The Power of Focus

Brahmacharya has often been misunderstood as celibacy, as the renunciation of pleasure and the denial of the senses. In the AXIS system, Brahmacharya reveals its true meaning: not denial, but discernment. Not restriction, but radiant, embodied clarity. It is the Power of Focus: the understanding that to live your most fulfilled, elevated, and ecstatic life, you must choose where to invest your most sacred resource: your time and your attention.

There are two foundational truths behind this Yama. The first is that time passes, and no matter how evolved or powerful you become, you will never retrieve the time you've lost. The second is that you can only experience one thing at a time. Consciousness requires an anchor of attention in order to exist as experience. Without attention, there is no perception, no continuity, no memory; there is no you. Reality is built on choice, and every choice you make defines the experience you will live and the one you won't.

This is the central revelation of Brahmacharya: **experience is exclusive**. Every time you say yes to one thing, you are saying no to infinite others. This is not something to fear, is something to *honor*. It means that your life is sculpted by your focus, and if the purpose of life is to enjoy, to feel, to participate in the miracle of creation through your own axis of becoming, then the most important question becomes: **What is the highest joy I am capable of experiencing?**

This is the yogic path: not to abstain from life, but to refine your relationship to pleasure. Not to diminish it, but to pursue it at its highest octave. Brahmacharya asks: What is the experience that fulfills you most deeply? What is the dream, the vision, the purpose that ignites your body, breath, mind and spirit?

Focus is not just mental: it is physical, emotional and energetic. It is the art of aligning your axis with what matters the most to you. This matters now more than ever.

In a world of hyperstimulation where cheap dopamine is available at every corner through social media, pornography, fast food and mindless consumption in all levels; we are being trained to disperse. To fragment. To trade meaning for excitement, fulfillment for addiction; but none of those things will ever give you what Brahmacharya promises: the sustained joy of embodied purpose.

Distraction is the biggest thief of your time and energy. Every hour spent in artificial pleasure is an hour not invested in becoming who you came here to be. Every moment of split attention is a vibration wasted, and once time passes, it never returns.

Brahmacharya invites you to flip the entire narrative: not to suppress pleasure, but to choose **only the highest pleasure**. The pleasure of alignment. The ecstasy of expression. The thrill of seeing your vision come to life.

That is the most intoxicating joy there is; to live your own dream. That dream cannot be downloaded; it must be built.

To live Brahmacharya is to ask yourself every day: *Is this experience worth my time? Is it feeding my becoming? Is it aligned with my axis?* If not, let it go. If yes, give it everything.

This is about self-direction. It's about living a life where every experience is intentional, and every moment is meaningful. When you live this way, your life becomes radiant. You shine with the clarity of purpose; you walk the earth as one who has chosen.

Through your focus, you generate the most valuable form of energy there is: **presence**. This is the power of Brahmacharya, this is the Power of Focus. Not to restrict life, but to direct it toward its most elevated form. To choose the highest pleasure, and to live it fully!

APARIGRAHA

अपरिग्रह

The Power of Release

Aparigraha is commonly translated as "non-possessiveness," but in the AXIS system, we don't define principles by what they are *not*. Instead, we explore what they *are*. Aparigraha is the Power of Release: a principle that teaches us to live in harmony with the natural movement of resonance, rather than against it. It is not about denying ownership. It is about recognizing that ownership is never the goal, alignment is!

To hold onto something tightly is to waste energy trying to control what cannot be controlled. Whether it's a relationship, a career, a phase of life, or an identity, the tighter you grip, the more tired you become. The purpose of experience is not to own it, but to **live it** fully while it's resonant, and to release it gracefully when the resonance fades.

This law applies across all domains of life. In family, friendship, romance, business, even in the way we relate to our pets or "belongings". Every relationship is based on an **energetic compatibility**. When that compatibility is high, the relationship is easeful, joyful, natural. When it fades, clinging does not restore it. It only creates friction, suffering, and loss of dignity.

Aparigraha teaches us to trust the **intelligence of space**. Just as we cannot hold our breath forever, we cannot hold experiences beyond their season. To release something is not to lose it, is to make room for what is now aligned. You don't need to chase what's meant for you, nor do you need to cling to what has served its purpose. The rhythm of life will always deliver what resonates with your current axis.

This doesn't mean you float through life with detachment; quite the opposite. It means you engage with full presence, knowing that the experience is sacred because it is impermanent. You give your all to participate, and when it's time to move on, you do so not in defeat, but in trust.

In truth, nothing is truly owned. **To own is to owe**. Every possession comes with responsibility, and if you haven't become the version of yourself capable of sustaining that responsibility, you will feel it as weight, not joy.

You don't have to refuse abundance, but you must learn to welcome it *without anxiety, without control, without fear of loss*. Because what is aligned will stay. What fades was never meant to be permanent.

Releasing is not the end of the cycle; it is the continuation of flow, it is the trust that with every ending comes a return to the void, where purification happens.

To practice Aparigraha is to live with deep presence, full engagement, and fearless surrender. It is the power to love without clinging, to experience without grasping, to walk with another without trying to own the path.

This is **the Power of Release**. The freedom to trust that what is yours cannot be taken, what leaves was never yours to hold.

In this way, Aparigraha becomes the final integration of the Yamas. It reminds us that nothing is permanent but the axis itself.

And now that the inner field has been refined, the next step arises naturally: to move through the world from this place of clarity. To enter into relationship with others, with society, and with the Earth.

By following these principles, we ensure that expanded perception leads to mastery, rather than confusion.

This is the path of the conscious mystic: the path into the limitless experience of reality.

For a mystic, it is not simply about ability, but about responsibility. It is not just about what you are capable of, but about the consequences of your actions, the ripples you send into the world.

We exist in a universe of cause and effect. Every action you take, every thought you hold, every breath you exhale creates a wave in the field of reality. So, as your power grows, so does your influence.

To walk this path is to understand that your presence is a force, and that force must be wielded with mastery. This is the mystic's law: to act with awareness, to walk with responsibility, to leave a trace of grace with every movement, every decision, every breath.

Study these laws. Study the Hermetic principles, the Chakras, the Yamas and Niyamas, and meditate upon them deeply. These are not merely concepts to understand but practices to embody. They will serve as your anchor in the vast ocean of consciousness, ensuring that as you expand, you remain steady, grounded, and sovereign over yourself.

CHAPTER XIII

THE AXIS ERA

The choice we make together

The future is bright. That is the vision I hold, the decision I commit myself to, and the direction of my creation. This is not wishful thinking; it is a choice. A choice to cultivate consciousness, coherence, and mastery over the Self. A choice to align with the expansion of human potential rather than its contraction. A choice to evolve, individually and collectively, toward a world where energy moves freely, knowledge is shared openly, and creativity flourishes without limitation.

When we awaken to the full power of our electromagnetic Self, when we embody the Axis system, we unlock a new kind of human experience: one that is ruled by abundance, collaboration, and inner sovereignty.

AXIS HUMAN:

The Axis human is one who has integrated their energy field; one who aligns posture, breath, and attention into a single, coherent force in conscious action. This being is:

- Physically strong, stable, and resilient, moving with efficiency and presence.

- Emotionally intelligent and balanced, able to process emotions without repression or impulsivity.
- Mentally sharp and focused, free from the distractions of external conditioning.
- Energetically vibrant, radiating vitality, enthusiasm, and presence.
- Creatively engaged, innovating in their craft, field, or artistic expression.
- Socially and environmentally conscious, aware of their impact and in harmony with the collective.

The Axis human is not just an individual force it is a center of connection, a magnet of energy that uplifts those around them.

Imagine a world where people live in full energetic integrity, where emotions do not dictate action but inform wisdom. Where thoughts are not chaotic but clear and intentional, where bodies are not weak and exhausted but strong and vital.

AXIS COMMUNITY

When a critical mass of individuals awakens their electromagnetic field, a new type of society begins to emerge. This is not an abstract utopia, but a natural result of higher levels of coherence within human systems.

With more people operating from full energetic sovereignty, we will see:

- An explosion of innovation: new forms of technology, architecture, and engineering based on sustainable and holistic design principles.

- A cultural renaissance: new styles of music, dance, clothing, and artistic expression as individuals tap into authentic and uninhibited creativity.
- A revolution in health and well-being, as people master their own energy systems and preventive health flourishes.
- The reinvention of food and agriculture; as consciousness expands, so does our relationship with nature; leading to cleaner, more efficient, and higher-frequency foods.
- The redefinition of education: new systems of inner education at an international scale, in which learning is no longer memorization and indoctrination, but an exploration of wisdom, creativity, and skill development.
- New economic models that emerge as more awakened creators, thinkers, and entrepreneurs explore the principles and applications of money and valuables. Resources flow toward meaningful innovation rather than extractive industries.

When energy flows freely within individuals, it begins to flow freely within society. When people connect more deeply with themselves, they connect more deeply with others. When we amplify our own frequency, we amplify the vibrational quality of the entire human collective.

This system and book are an invitation into transformation, so we can define what is possible as a collective. A community and a world where science and mysticism, technology and nature, logic and intuition, are not opposing forces; but complementary expressions of a greater whole.

THE AGE OF SELF-REALIZATION

This is the revolution I commit myself to: a revolution of expansion, of self-mastery, of true human potential. A world where we are not passive spectators of our existence, but active participants in the great unfolding of life.

A world where we replace warfare with welfare, division with collaboration, fear with knowledge, stagnation with expansion.

A world where each individual holds their own axis, their own sovereign field of energy, mastery over body, mind, and reality.

This is the Era of the Axis Human.

This is our path forward.

THE VISION FOR A NEW REALITY

We have traveled far. We have explored the foundations of the Self: the alignment of posture, breath, and attention. We have awakened the Chakra system, the structure of the energy body, and learned how to move energy through it with precision to master our vital force.

We have expanded into Pratyahara, the integration of the senses, and opened the gateway to higher perception, we have taken our first steps into the mystic state with the grace and knowledge of the Niyamas and Yamas.

Now, we must ask the ultimate question:

What do we do with this knowledge?

This book has not been about philosophy for philosophy's sake. It has not been about awakening for personal indulgence. It has been about action, about movement, about creating something real from what we have discovered.

And this leads us to the final step…

THE VISION:

The Axis System is a blueprint for a new kind of human experience, a new kind of society, a new kind of world. We are stepping into an era of extraordinary possibility. Technology is advancing at an exponential rate, the world is shifting, breaking, reforming itself at a speed never seen.

In the middle of this great transformation, we have a choice: We can allow ourselves to be carried by the tides of history, just as passive observers of a world shaped by others, or we can take our place as conscious creators. As architects of a future that is not only technologically advanced, but spiritually awakened.

THE FUTURE IS BRIGHT!

Not because we wait for it to be so…

BUT BECAUSE WE CHOOSE TO MAKE IT SO.

SO MOTE IT IS.

GLOSSARY

1. **Axis (uppercase):** Refers to the system, methodology and living framework presented in this book.

2. **axis (lowercase):** An imaginary central line around which a system, object, or concept is organized or rotates; often used symbolically to indicate balance or orientation.

3. **Anapana Sati:** A traditional Buddhist meditation practice focused on the mindful awareness of natural breathing to cultivate concentration and clarity.

4. **Bio-electromagnetism:** The study of electrical and magnetic processes produced by living organisms, such as neural signals and cardiac rhythms.

5. **Biofield:** A field of energy and information surrounding and permeating living systems, used in integrative health frameworks.

6. **Biophoton:** Light emissions produced by biological systems, associated with cellular metabolic processes.

7. **Collective Mind:** The shared patterns of thought, beliefs, perceptions within a group, culture, or society.

8. **Conscious Mind:** The aspect of yourself that is responsible of intentional thought, perception, decision-making, and attention in the present moment.

9. **Default Mode Network (DMN):** A network of brain regions active during rest and self-referential thinking, such as daydreaming, memory recall, and self-reflection.

10. **Electromagnetic Field:** A physical field produced by combining electric and magnetic forces.

11. **Endocrine System:** A network of glands that release hormones to regulate growth, metabolism, mood, reproduction, and homeostasis.

12. **Enteric Nervous System (ENS):** A complex network of neurons in the gastrointestinal tract that controls digestion and communicates with the brain.

13. **Fibonacci Sequence:** A numerical pattern in which each number is the sum of the two preceding ones, commonly found in natural growth patterns.

14. **Golden Ratio (Phi):** A mathematical proportion (~1.618) associated with aesthetic harmony and observed in nature, art, and architecture.

15. **Hatha Raja Yoga:** A synthesis of physical postures (Hatha) and mental discipline (Raja) aimed at preparing the body and mind for meditation.

16. **Individuation:** A psychological process described by Carl Jung as the integration of the conscious and unconscious aspects of the Self.

17. **Japa:** A meditative practice involving the repetitive recitation of a mantra to cultivate focus and inner awareness.

18. **Kabbalah:** A mystical tradition within Judaism that explores the nature of existence, consciousness, and the divine through symbolic systems.

19. **Mandala:** A geometric or symbolic design representing wholeness, often used as a tool for meditation and contemplation.

20. **Matter Field:** A theoretical term referring to the physical manifestation of energy as particles or matter within space-time.

21. **Metabolic Efficiency:** The ability of an organism to convert nutrients into usable energy with minimal waste.

22. **Metatron's Cube:** A sacred geometry figure derived from the Flower of Life, containing base geometric pattern associated with spatial structure.

23. **Parasympathetic Nervous System:** A branch of the autonomic nervous system responsible for rest, digestion, and recovery.

24. **Path to the Self:** The commitment or covenant to become your most authentic Self trough every action in coherence with your purpose, intention and mission.

25. **Pineal Gland:** A small endocrine gland in the center of the brain that regulates biological timing. It produces melatonin for circadian rhythm, sleep, and appetite regulation, synthesizes serotonin for mood and metabolic signaling, while it has been associated with endogenous DMT.

26. **Pituitary Gland:** Often called the "master gland," it regulates other endocrine glands and influences growth, stress, and reproduction.

27. **Proprioception:** Is your body's subconscious sense of its own position, movement, and effort in space, relying on receptors in muscles, joints, and tendons to send signals to the brain, allowing for balance, coordinated movement.

28. **Prefrontal Cortex:** The brain region involved in executive functions such as planning, reasoning, emotional regulation, and decision-making.

29. **Psyche:** The totality of the human narrative and mind, including conscious and unconscious processes.

30. **Psychosomatic:** Describing the interaction between psychological and emotional factors with physical health and vitality.

31. **Quantum Computer:** A type of computer that uses quantum bits (qubits) to perform calculations based on quantum mechanical principles, this is the most advanced computer mechanism known to men.

32. **Quantum Field:** A fundamental concept in physics describing the pre-matter state: fields that underlie particles and forces at the smallest scales.

33. **Sacred Geometry:** A symbolic mathematic system of geometry that reflects the main patterns underlying nature and existence.

34. **Sacred Technology:** A term used to describe tools or practices intended to enhance awareness, coherence with the divine, and well-being.

35. **Seed and Flower of Life:** Geometric patterns composed of overlapping circles, symbolizing the perfect symmetry of creation and the interconnectedness between all things.

36. **self (lowercase):** The everyday, personal identity formed by memories, roles, beliefs, emotions, and self-narratives; it is shaped by experience, culture, and conditioning; it operates within ordinary conscious awareness.

37. **Self (uppercase):** The unified essence; the integrative force that unifies, and organizes all the aspects and components of what we are, both mental, physical and spiritual. It represents wholeness, coherence, and authenticity beyond transient roles or narratives; in Jungian psychology it refers to the unifying center that integrates the conscious and unconscious.

38. **Self-image:** The idea one has of one's abilities, appearance, and personality. An individual's self-image is developed over time and influenced by the experiences they have encountered.

39. **Self-mastery:** The ability to regulate one's thoughts, emotions, and behaviors in alignment with personal values and goals.

40. **Self-narrative:** The internal story individuals construct about their identity, experiences, and life meaning.

41. **Self-realization:** The process of recognizing one's true nature, potential, and purpose.

42. **Sensorimotor Spectrum:** The range between sensory input and motor responses involved in perception and physical interaction with the environment (aka. Consciousness).

43. **Signature Vibration:** An individual's unique pattern of inner energetic dynamic and outer behavioral expression.

44. **Soma:** The living body as experienced from within, emphasizing felt bodily awareness rather than anatomy alone.

45. **Somatic Studies:** An interdisciplinary field created by Thomas Hanna that focused on bodily perception, movement, and embodied experience.

46. **Sovereignty:** The capacity for self-governance, autonomy, and responsibility over one's inner and outer life.

47. **Star of David:** A six-pointed geometric symbol formed by two interlocking triangles, commonly associated with Judaism and balance.

48. **Subconscious:** Processes of experience operating below conscious awareness that influence shadow behavior, deep emotions, unhealed trauma and compulsive habits.

49. **Superconscious:** A state of awareness beyond ordinary self-referential thought, associated with insight, creativity, and meaning-making. In Nietzsche's philosophy, it can be understood as operating beyond conditioned morality and ego narratives, engaging higher values, and self-transcendence.

50. **Sympathetic Nervous System:** A branch of the autonomic nervous system responsible for activating the body's responses.

51. **Toroidal Field:** A doughnut-shaped energy or magnetic field pattern observed in physics and biological models.

52. **Trataka:** A yogic concentration practice involving steady gazing at a fixed point to improve focus and mental clarity.

53. **Unified Energy Field (U.E.F.):** A framework proposing that all matter and energy arise from a single interconnected field.

54. **Vagus Nerve:** A major cranial nerve that connects the brain to the heart, lungs, and digestive system, influencing relaxation and regulation.

55. **Vibrational Frequency:** The rate of oscillation of a wave or system; metaphorically used to describe the dynamic or intensity of energy or behavior.

REFERENCES

1. **American Psychological Association.** (2017). *Stress in America: The State of Our Nation.* APA.

2. **Balban, M. Y.,** DeSouza, D. D., Wirth, M., Freed, J., Anaclet, C., Panas, D., … & Breathing-Based Treatment Consortium. (2023). "Brief structured respiration practices enhance mood and reduce physiological arousal." *Cell Reports Medicine*, 4(2), 100891.

3. **Baliki, M. N.,** Geha, P. Y., Apkarian, A. V., & Chialvo, D. R. (2010). "Beyond feeling: Chronic pain hurts the brain, disrupting the default-mode network dynamics." *Journal of Neuroscience*, 30(4), 1398–1403.

4. **Becker, R. O., & Selden, G.** (1985). *The Body Electric: Electromagnetism and the Foundation of Life.* Harper.

5. **Brewer, J. A.,** Worhunsky, P. D., Gray, J. R., Tang, Y.-Y., Weber, J., & Kober, H. (2011). "Meditation experience is associated with differences in default mode network activity and connectivity." *Proceedings of the National Academy of Sciences*, 108(50), 20254–20259.

6. **Buzsáki, G.** (2006). *Rhythms of the Brain.* Oxford University Press.

7. **Cao, B.,** Benda, N. C., Henke, R., & Warburton, D. (2023). "Postural alignment and metabolic efficiency: Investigating energy expenditure and muscle recruitment." *BMC Public Health*, 23(16617).

8. **Carney, D. R.,** Cuddy, A. J. C., & Yap, A. J. (2010). "Power posing: Brief nonverbal displays affect neuroendocrine levels and risk tolerance." *Psychological Science*, 21(10), 1363–1368.

9. **Damour, L.** (2019). *Under Pressure: Confronting the Epidemic of Stress and Anxiety in Girls.* Ballantine Books.

10. **Davidson, R. J., & McEwen, B. S.** (2012). "Social influences on neuroplasticity: Stress and interventions to promote well-being." *Nature Neuroscience*, 15(5), 689–695.

11. **Dispenza, J.** (2019). *Becoming Supernatural: How Common People Are Doing the Uncommon.* Hay House Inc.

12. **Dispenza, J.** (2014). *Breaking the Habit of Being Yourself: How to Lose Your Mind and Create a New One.* Hay House Inc.

13. **Einstein, A.** (1954). *Ideas and Opinions.* Crown Publishing Group.

14. **Fornari, M.,** Shafer, H., & Patel, S. (2017). "Spinal alignment and vagal nerve stimulation: Implications for digestive health." *Journal of Gastrointestinal Neurology*, 14(3), 217–225.

15. **Gandhi, M.** (1927). *The Story of My Experiments with Truth.* Navajivan Publishing House.

16. **Gershon, M. D.** (1999). *The Second Brain: The Scientific Basis of Gut Instinct and a Groundbreaking New Understanding of Nervous Disorders of the Stomach and Intestine.* Harper.

17. **Goyal, M.,** Singh, S., Sibinga, E. M. S., Gould, N. F., Rowland-Seymour, A., Sharma, R., & Haythornthwaite, J. A. (2014). "Meditation programs for psychological stress and well-being." *JAMA Internal Medicine,* 174(3), 357–368.

18. **Haidt, J.** (2012). *The Righteous Mind: Why Good People Are Divided by Politics and Religion.* Pantheon Books.

19. **Hanna, T.** (1988). *Somatics: Reawakening the Mind's Control of Movement, Flexibility, and Health.* Addison-Wesley.

20. **Harris, T.** (2019). *How to Build a Humane Technology.* Center for Humane Technology.

21. **Hebb, D. O.** (1949). *The Organization of Behavior: A Neuropsychological Theory.* Wiley.

22. **Heraclitus.** (trans. various). *Fragments.* (Original work c. 500 BCE).

23. **Huberman, A.** (2021). "Breathwork protocols for health, focus, and stress." *Huberman Lab Podcast.*

24. **Huberman, A.** (2023). *Protocols: An Operating Manual for the Human Body.* Penguin Press.

25. **Huxley, A.** (1954). *The Doors of Perception.* Harper & Brothers.

26. **Jerath, R.,** Edry, J. W., Barnes, V. A., & Jerath, V. (2006). "Physiology of long pranayamic breathing." *Medical Hypotheses,* 67(3), 566–571.

27. **Jha, A. P.** (2021). *Peak Mind: Find Your Focus, Own Your Attention.* HarperOne.

28. **Jung, C. G.** (1959). *The Archetypes and the Collective Unconscious.* Princeton University Press.

29. **Jung, C. G.** (1964). *Man and His Symbols.* Doubleday.

30. **Krishnamurti, J.** (1954). *The First and Last Freedom.* Harper & Brothers.

31. **Lao Tzu.** (trans. various). *Tao Te Ching.* (Original work c. 6th century BCE).

32. **Lazar, S. W.,** Kerr, C. E., Wasserman, R. H., Gray, J. R., Greve, D. N., & Treadway, M. T. (2005). "Meditation experience is associated with increased cortical thickness." *NeuroReport*, 16(17), 1893–1897.

33. **Lee, H. J., & Lee, W. C.** (2019). "The effect of cervical posture on pulmonary function." *Journal of Physical Therapy Science*, 31(7), 542–545.

34. **Lembke, A.** (2021). *Dopamine Nation: Finding Balance in the Age of Indulgence*. Dutton.

35. **Levitin, D. J.** (2014). *The Organized Mind*. Dutton.

36. **Lipton, B. H.** (2005). *The Biology of Belief*. Hay House.

37. **Livio, M.** (2002). *The Golden Ratio*. Broadway Books.

38. **Manning, J. T., & Pickup, L. J.** (1998). "Symmetry and performance in competitive sports." *Journal of Anatomy*, 192(4), 547–553.

39. **Maté, G.** (2003). *When the Body Says No*. Knopf Canada.

40. **McCraty, R.,** Atkinson, M., & Bradley, R. T. (2009). "Electrophysiological evidence of intuition." *Journal of Alternative and Complementary Medicine*, 15(1), 15–27.

41. **McCraty, R.,** Atkinson, M., & Bradley, R. T. (2014). *Electrophysiological Evidence of Intuition*. HeartMath Institute.

42. **McEwen, B. S.** (2002). *The End of Stress As We Know It*. Dana Press.

43. **McKenna, T.** (1992). *Food of the Gods*. Bantam Books.

44. **Nair, S.,** Sagar, M., Sollers, J., Consedine, N. S., & Broadbent, E. (2015). "The effect of postural changes on stress responses." *Health Psychology*, 34(6), 635–641.

45. **Patanjali.** (1978). *The Yoga Sutras of Patanjali* (trans. Swami Satchidananda). Integral Yoga Publications.

46. **Patanjali.** (2009). *The Yoga Sutras of Patanjali* (trans. Edwin F. Bryant). North Point Press.

47. **Porges, S. W.** (2011). *The Polyvagal Theory*. W. W. Norton & Company.

48. **Posner, M. I.** (2012). *Attention in a Social World*. Oxford University Press.

49. **Posner, M. I., & Petersen, S. E.** (1990). "The attention system of the human brain." *Annual Review of Neuroscience*, 13(1), 25–42.

50. **Popp, F. A.** (1992). "Biophoton emission." *Journal of Photochemistry and Photobiology B*, 14(3), 357–375.

51. **Ram Dass.** (1971). *Be Here Now*. Crown Publishing Group.

52. **Riskind, J. H., & Gotay, C. C.** (1982). "Physical posture." *Cognition & Emotion*, 46(1), 103–113.

53. **Rubik, B.** (2002). *The Biofield Hypothesis. Journal of Alternative and Complementary Medicine*.

54. **Rumi.** (1995). *The Essential Rumi* (trans. Coleman Barks). HarperCollins.

55. **Sadhguru.** (2016). *Inner Engineering*. Spiegel & Grau.

56. **Santomauro, D. F., et al.** (2021). *Global Prevalence and Burden of Depressive and Anxiety Disorders. JAMA Psychiatry*.

57. **Schacter, D. L.,** Addis, D. R., & Buckner, R. L. (2007). "The prospective brain." *Nature Reviews Neuroscience*, 8(9), 657–661.

58. **Strassman, R.** (2001). *DMT: The Spirit Molecule*. Park Street Press.

59. **The Three Initiates.** (1908). *The Kybalion*. Yogi Publication Society.

60. **Watts, A.** (1957). *The Way of Zen*. Pantheon Books.

61. **World Health Organization.** (2022). *World Mental Health Report*. WHO Press.

62. **Zaccaro, A.,** Piarulli, A., Laurino, M., Garbella, E., Menicucci, D., Neri, B., & Gemignani, A. (2018). "How breath-control can change your life." *Frontiers in Human Neuroscience*, 12, 353.

63. **Zaccaro, A.,** Scattolin, M., Garbella, E., Gennai, S., & Gemignani, A. (2022). "Psychophysiological and clinical correlates of slow breathing." *Scientific Reports*, 12(1), 27247.

AXIS SYSTEM

THE PATH TO THE SELF.

ORIGINAL BY SAMUEL TOBON CASTAÑO.

2025

.

www.ingramcontent.com/pod-product-compliance
Lightning Source LLC
Chambersburg PA
CBHW051616120626
46551CB00014B/1819